PELICAN BOOKS

A930

HUMANISM

H. J. Blackham left school early – and with a passion for horses – to work on a farm in the Midlands. Later he entered the honours school of English at the University of Birmingham. After a year's post-graduate study he taught for two years at Doncaster Grammar School. By now his main interest had switched to philosophy, and with it he turned to adult education, and to London. During the war he served in the London Fire Brigade, and was a liaison officer with the Port of London Authority during the preparations for D-Day. After the war he became secretary of the Ethical Union and of the International Humanist and Ethical Union on its formation in 1952. He became Director of the British Humanist Association when this was formed in 1963.

His books include *Six Existentialist Thinkers* (1952), *The Human Tradition* (1953), *Political Discipline in a Free Society* (1961), and *Religion in a Modern Society* (1966). He has also contributed to *A History of Freedom of Thought* by J. B. Bury (1952), *Reality, Man and Existence* (1965), and *Objections to Humanism*, which is available as a Pelican. He is editor of a forthcoming series of studies in the history of ideas.

H. J. BLACKHAM

HUMANISM

*

PENGUIN BOOKS

Penguin Books Ltd, Harmondsworth, Middlesex, England
Penguin Books Inc., 3300 Clipper Mill Road, Baltimore, Md 21211, U.S.A.
Penguin Books Australia Ltd, Ringwood, Victoria, Australia

—

First published 1968

—

Copyright © H. J. Blackham, 1968

—

Made and printed in Great Britain
by Richard Clay (The Chaucer Press) Ltd,
Bungay, Suffolk
Set in Monotype Imprint

Dedicated to the memory
of Democritus and
Protagoras *et alii*

CONTENTS

PREFACE

THE hasty non-reader looking for humanism on a postcard who happens to pick up this book is advised to glance over the first chapter and, time and wind allowing, to go on in the same manner over chapters four, seven and ten. These are not the most important chapters nor the best written, but together they might best answer the demand for potted humanism. I hope that the book as a whole shows why any potted version is without flavour. All the same, it is a structured humanism I have set out to describe, the humanism which humanists share, not my humanism.

At times the reader may think that I am not writing about humanism at all but about, say, society or Christianity. For humanism is about the world, not about humanism. It would be perfectly possible to write about humanism without a mention of Christianity, but in this country with centuries of Christian tradition and a Christian establishment, that would be irresponsible. Humanism in Europe or America has to be in a preliminary way justification of a rejection of Christianity. In other cultures also humanism has been the alternative to the dominant religious outlook. Indeed, humanism is the permanent alternative to religion, an essentially different way of taking and tackling human life in the world.

Humanism is the human case and the human cause, an age-old conviction about the human case now slowly coming into its own which will induce men and women in number to espouse the human cause with head and heart and with two hands.

No construction, however broadly based, will have an *absolute* authority; the indomitable freedom of life to be more, to be new, to be what it has not entered into the heart of man as yet to conceive, must always remain standing. With that freedom goes the modesty of reason that can lay claim only to partial knowledge, and to the ordering of a particular soul, or city, or civilization.

GEORGE SANTAYANA

I

PRELIMINARIES

It is unreasonableness not to submit to the necessary
conditions of life.
People are fools who live without enjoyment of life.
Democritus

Assumptions

HUMANISM proceeds from an assumption *that* man is on his
own and this life is all and an assumption *of* responsibility for
one's own life and for the life of mankind – an appraisal and an
undertaking, two personal decisions. Less than this is never
humanism. And this is only a skeleton, a personal frame, but
not the person.

There are four far-reaching independent assumptions here,
each of which needs to be justified. Although independent,
taken together they sketch a rudimentary view of man in the
world and prescribe the rudiments of a way of life dependent
upon it. All humanists as humanists accept the description
and the prescription, but, because both are rudimentary,
humanists do differ widely in the shape they give to them in
fashioning for themselves their view of the world and their
way of life. What they keep in common is this set of underlying assumptions. They have them in common today and they
have them in common with humanists of the near past and the
far past.

These assumptions, though crude and needing to be justified
and to be refined, are not vague. They are so definite and
decisive that they divide mankind, now and in the past. There
have been and there are humanist and non-humanist lives and
philosophies, distinguished by acceptance or refusal of these
assumptions.

Must humanists to be humanists hold all four of these
assumptions? Suppose I leave the first two as open questions
and concentrate on the practical undertakings, am I not a

good humanist, all the better for being open minded? Perhaps, but this does imply an assumption of the first two propositions in practice, which demands just as much justification as the explicit assumption.

What of the person who makes the two first assumptions but refuses or does not bother to take on responsibility? This is not illogical. The acceptance of responsibility is not a necessary inference from the assumption that man is on his own and this life is all. I might shrug off responsibility, saying, 'I did not ask to be born', perhaps adding, 'anyhow, my lot in life is not worth having'. Having reached years of discretion, one might look round and conclude that human life on these conditions was not worth living, and decide on suicide. Or the same conclusion might lead to reckless living. All this does happen. Indeed, the common thought of those who do not believe that man is on his own and this life is all is just this, that if they did believe it they would see no reason to live responsibly at all. A choice is involved here, a basic choice of life for which one makes oneself responsible, or a refusal. The refusal of responsibility without a refusal of life is certainly possible, and it is not uncommon. But it is not humanism.

The first two assumptions are plain and definite enough, but the notion of responsibility gives some difficulty. Strictly, one is responsible to someone for something. If not responsible to God, to whom is man responsible? Who will make him accountable if there is no last Day? The notion of 'man' also gives difficulty, since we deal only with men and women and 'man' is often used to mean more than the species mankind. All the same, there is a recognizable sense in which responsibility may be real without meaning accountability to another to whom one is answerable. One speaks of 'making oneself responsible for', and this is not to be given responsibility by another to whom one is made accountable, but to take it upon oneself and thus to make oneself answerable to oneself. That this may be a real and solemn undertaking cannot seriously be doubted. Sanctions which responsibility always involves apply in this case also, for there is no more painful condition than to be self-condemned.

One may, then, properly take on responsibility for one's own life and for the life of mankind although one is not accountable to any higher authority, but it is still not clear just what one is in this case responsible for. Is it a limited or an unlimited responsibility? The Stoics limited responsibility. Over events one had no power and therefore no responsibility for them. Over one's own dispositions and responses and actions one had full power and therefore total responsibility for them. This was a neat division into inside and outside, with full control and responsibility in the one area and none in the other. This does not fit the modern human situation: we know too much and can do too much to accept this account of human responsibility. On the other hand, Jean-Paul Sartre makes every man totally responsible for everything, whatever he does about anything. This is merely rhetorical, or so alarming that one gives up. The truth of experience seems to be that one cannot set limits to one's responsibility for oneself and for others and for events; and that at the same time one has to set practical limits in order to be able to do anything effective at all. Humanists cannot possibly discharge the responsibility they take on; like others, they can only do their best and strive to do better, steering between complacency and demoralization and despair. Life is always an untidy and risky business, and in taking on responsibility for it one is bound to accept this along with the other inescapable conditions.

The notion of responsibility of course includes also the assumption that we have the power to will something and to carry it out, that we are not puppets, not totally subject to influences without and within outside our control which determine what we are and what we do. Justification of 'free-will' has occasioned even more pages of inconclusive argument than justification of belief in an external world. What Santayana has called 'animal faith' is the short way with both problems, and in the end the only way. However, the really important point about the freedom of our decisions and actions is that they are never free in the sense of uncaused and that they need not be wholly determined by inside drives and outside constraints over which we have no control and of which we may have no knowledge. That is to say, self-determination is possible and its scope can be enlarged. This increasing control in personal life and in the life of mankind is the perspective of humanism.

One further point: to take on responsibility, to make oneself responsible for one's own life and for the life of mankind sounds safe and solid, but no doubt Hitler saw fit to exterminate the Jews with a good conscience in a responsible manner because he found good reasons for so doing. Is humanist responsibility merely subjective? Does humanism not stand with all the higher religions in upholding an objective universal standard? Do humanists not acknowledge any rule of conduct that is obligatory, binding on conscience?

Humanism is not original here where it would be inhuman to be original. Humanists do not dissent from the consensus of mankind down the ages on basic practical moral questions. The rough summary of this is doing to others as we would be done to, the Gospel injunction which Hobbes universalizes by turning it into the more cautious negative form: do not do to another what you do not want done to yourself. The more sophisticated Kantian version makes it a categorical imperative to treat human being in oneself and in any other person always as an end, never as merely a means. Modern existentialists reaffirm the same principle in the I–thou relationship which subsists between all human beings as equal subjects, although ever liable to be degraded by the subordination of one as merely an object to the other. However this ultimate moral relationship of equality as human beings is expressed, and whatever theoretical justification for it is found, humanists are on the side of the angels in upholding the principle at stake. Indeed, this is the fundamental humanism: man as an end. This is the clue to the great labyrinth, which makes humanism a simple deliverance.

However, it is distinctively a humanist contribution to recognize that it is not enough to accept this prescript and try to act on it, for it is not unconditional. Hobbes points out that it would not be reasonable to practise it in 'the state of nature', for that would be to make oneself a victim, which one cannot be required to do. It becomes reasonable only in a society which gives one security from one's neighbour. The social contract which delivered man from the state of nature is a useful myth, but the point that morality exists only in a society and is a function of that society and not an independent absolute is a fact of fundamental importance. Morality as a universal absolute is a pernicious myth. The conditions of society are the conditions of morality. When that has been said, it remains the aspiration of the humanist *to be able* to make man an end, in every person.

Justifications

These large assumptions from which humanism proceeds need justification. Although they are only beginnings, presuppositions, they are the end of what may be a long argument. Humanists do not make such assumptions carelessly nor arbitrarily; they feel they are required to make them. Why?

That man is on his own and this life is all cannot be established once for all for one and all: these are not scientifically verifiable propositions. Each has to come to his own conclusions about them for himself. That is to say, everyone has to make his own assessment of the evidence and of the claims of alternative views. Of course these assumptions are contrary to the beliefs of most men at most times, but they are what some men have thought at some times, they are strongly indicated by the natural history of man as now known, and humanists do not find convincing the evidence for contrary beliefs. Fuller treatment of the question will follow in the next chapter. Here the point to be made is that the onus of justification has shifted from those who make these assumptions to those who dare to make contrary assumptions in the face of the natural history of man as now known. Although it is true that these are large assumptions which require justification and that they are the conclusions of a long argument which perhaps can never be fully conclusive, the ground argument has been going on over the years in connexion with evolutionary theory, and the gist of it is generally accepted;

so that it is the religious view of man which has to be accommodated to the biological understanding of man; the onus has shifted. At least, the humanist argues that it has.

The practical assumption of responsibility for one's own life and for the life of mankind, on the initial assumption that man is on his own, needs another kind of justification. Perhaps it is only a refusal to make oneself responsible that requires justification. But the decision to take on responsibility may be gloomy or exhilarating, according to one's estimate of the prospects for oneself or for mankind. This uncovers another root of humanism, besides the set of four primary assumptions. For nobody is going to take on sovereign responsibility unless he feels that it is worth while. What justifies this undertaking?

Everyone makes his own vital response to the world, weak or strong. One may be seized from behind by the poetry of things (as well as on the road to Damascus); one may be excited by an artist or an art or by all of the arts or by a science or a scientific vision of the world; one may see in the face of the natural world in all its seasons and moods an ultimate consolation; heaven may be other people; one may be in love; for some there is the loved monotony of sweet familiar things or the unfailing stimulus of the daily scene and common round. Of course this is the bright side. There is the reverse, and there is the waning or withering of vital response or its desolating surcease. Both aspects represent our common experience as human beings, and it is in the plenitude of this experience that humanism has its main root. One must be bound to the world by some bonds of love or respond to it with some excitement or enthusiasm before humanism can help one. Humanism is not a substitute for this spontaneous response, and is helpless without it. This mixed personal response to the world of hope and fear, love and hate, is the raw material to which humanism gives a definite shape and which again is finished off by the person for himself. What humanism can and cannot do in this intermediate role is the subject of the book, not to be anticipated here, but it should be stressed now that its role is intermediary; it does not furnish nor change the raw material and it does not finish the product. The single theme of humanism is self-determination, for persons, for groups and societies, for mankind together. Illumination of this theme is the perpetual business of humanism, and aid in translating it into practice. The set of primary assumptions justifies the theme and launches it as the human enterprise, but it is kept buoyant and carried forward by the zests which flow from personal interests, passions, pursuits, visions. Humanism is a certain kind of attachment to the world and a certain manner of participation in it.

Humanists without Knowing It

As a result of some common experience of life and reflection upon it people may find themselves in the humanist position. Contact with others who have followed the same course may reinforce their position. That is, before further reflection refines upon it and justifies it and makes it fully consistent with itself, humanism is a position in which people find themselves. When it is held up for all to see and made explicit, people who would not for themselves have been articulate about it are liable to say, with pardonable exaggeration, 'Then I have been a humanist all my life without knowing it.'

As a view of the world and a way of life which people may come to for themselves without giving it a name, humanism is more 'natural' than the 'higher' religions with a body of specific doctrines and practices that have to be learned. At the same time it is usually thought that man is naturally religious, that humanist assumptions are never entertained by natural man. However, there is no point in trying to distinguish between what is natural and what is cultural, for both religion and humanism are cultural, and there is no 'natural' man. The point worth making is that the elements of humanism are found even in primitive societies and are found in advanced forms in the advanced civilizations of long ago. It is natural in this sense of universal, liable to be found anywhere, and to develop where conditions are favourable, not a far-fetched nor a sophisticated way of looking at things which could never occur to ordinary people.

Although one may be a good humanist without knowing it, and certainly without wearing the badge of any organization, that does not mean that there is nothing to be learned from an articulate and explicit humanism and nothing to be gained by joining an organization. Humanism is a teaching, an education in living and an organization of help in practice.

Kinds of Humanism

There are two distinct ways in which there are different kinds of humanism. There are different uses of the name, for example, literary humanism and Christian humanism, and there are different kinds of person who make different kinds of humanist although they share the set of primary assumptions from which humanism proceeds.

Obviously, if humanism is said to proceed from the assumption that man is on his own and this life is all no Christian is a humanist in that sense. Having said this, one remembers a few who call themselves Christians who *are* humanists in that sense but find their inspiration in the Christian way of life which they choose, accepting the help of myth, symbol and ritual to support their practice of it. This is one kind of person who makes one kind of humanist, just as another kind finds his inspiration in a cosmic scientific vision which kindles his imagination and stirs him to embrace the world with a warmth that duty and responsibility could never rouse in him, because he is made to feel that man is promethean, a significant part of a creative universe. The humanist who chooses to call himself a Christian and practise the Christian way of life without the support of the Christian faith is an extreme case, but the name 'Christian humanist' has meaning in the sense of this chapter in so far as it approximates to this case. Mostly, Christians do not mean this when they use the name. They usually mean a Christian who gives full value to human life in this world and allows it a relative autonomy, and who does so because in his belief it is God's world and a God-given autonomy. The contrast is with a fundamentalist preoccupation with salvation or with an other-worldly focus of interest.

Literary humanism is the humanism associated with the European rediscovery of Greek and Latin literature at the Renaissance. The humanists were the scholars who devoted themselves to these studies. Hence the term 'humanities' has been used in the universities for the arts, the non-scientific subjects. To use humanism currently in the historical sense of literary culture is more confusing than useful.

Sometimes the term 'scientific humanism' is used, perhaps to distinguish modern humanism from literary humanism and from religious humanism, perhaps because the humanists who use it want to put the accent on their scientific attitude. This is fair enough when the term is used personally, but 'scientific humanism' is far, far too narrow for the modern humanism oriented on development which claims the whole human inheritance and would employ all human resources. Besides, any term which suggests a blithe ignorance of the nature and limits of rational thinking is not good enough for a full-blooded humanism.

A 'full-blooded humanism' may seem to contradict what I have been saying, for it suggests a fully worked-out humanist philosophy, a view of the world and a way of life described and prescribed in detail, whereas I have been saying that the humanism which all humanists have in common is a certain set of assumptions and a certain undertaking – bones not blood. Leading humanists are likely to teach a philosophy of their own in which they believe and by which they live, and this will be a full-blooded exemplary personal humanism likely to inspire and help many people. Sir Julian Huxley is a notable contemporary instance. There are other hardly remembered names of a generation ago. Humanism exists only in the personal thought and lives of humanists, but they exemplify and dispense *a* humanism, not humanism. One of the best-known expositions of Sartre's existentialism, though not the best, has the title 'Existentialism is a Humanism'. Sartre's own existentialism is a humanism. Gabriel Marcel's is not. There are humanist philosophies and non-humanist philosophies, but humanism is not a particular philosophy. If it had been it would have died and been embalmed in the history of philosophy. Technical philosophy is concerned with epistemology, ontology, axiology, ethics, metaphysics and such special disciplines. Humanism is immediately concerned with decisive answers to questions that will not wait for the resolution of puzzles and the settlement of age-old disputes. As theology does not invent Christianity but serves to formulate and to defend it, so the philosophies may be used to attack or to defend the blunt position of those who according to their lights and what they feel in their bones find themselves constrained to think that man is on his own and this life is all, and who go on to conclude that nevertheless human values are worth all the endeavour they exact.

By a 'full-blooded humanism' I also meant a reminder that humanism is not merely a plea for rationality but also a recognition and acceptance of all sides of human nature and an acknowledged responsibility for employing all resources on human development.

Popular Humanism

Humanism as a stubborn delivery of common sense is all very well until the questions are raised which make it look perhaps less sensible than was thought. These questions in turn raise their own questions, and one is engaged on the terrain of philosophy. There is, however, a wider humanism which promises to unite more people and to provoke fewer questions.

Many people are not prepared to say that man is on his own and this life is all. They want to keep an open mind on such big questions, or they may believe the contraries, more or less. At the same time, they think these are questions which can be left to take care of themselves, so to speak. There is little or nothing we can do about them. What we can and must do is to tackle the problems which confront us here and now as human beings engaged in living on this planet. For the first time in its history mankind has been brought together by global problems which affect everybody and which can be effectively tackled only by the cooperation of all the peoples and by means of the increasingly available resources for dealing with practical problems. International security, the population explosion, the need to conserve resources, the needs of developing peoples: here is the sample of grave but not hopeless problems which threaten all humanity and with which the scientific revolution promises a new order of help. There is a common humanity with a common programme as never before, and questions of human nature and destiny are to be settled practically by getting on with this programme, rather than speculatively or by the acceptance or rejection of traditional beliefs.

There are many and will be more who feel in this way, however inarticulately. They are seized by the importance of the practical problems and the practical possibilities. Religious questions they regard as matters of opinion or matters of private concern. They are bored by any attempt to make issues of them or controversy about them; this is old-fashioned and unnecessary. There is no way of settling them, and they are no longer a matter of public concern: this is focused on the human task, in terms of problems to be dealt with and possibilities to be realized – or avoided.

This popular humanism, although it is in some respects naïve and blind, may find a quite sophisticated leadership among the technocrats. Humanists as defined in this chapter are completely in sympathy with the priority given to the human programme. They are not dissatisfied because these popular humanists do not and will not chant: 'Man is on his own, this life is all.' They are dissatisfied because without some clearer and fuller vision of society and of personal life there is nothing to guide the programme. Not only first and last questions but also human virtues and values are left to take care of themselves. Therefore humanists in the narrower but fuller sense would aspire to give the leadership to this popular humanism that would otherwise fall to the technocrats.* In

* The day after I had written this paragraph there was a special article in *The Times* by Imre Vajda, professor of economics at Budapest University, in which he wrote of the Common Market: 'The idea of union in its contemporary form is an idea of technocrats, not of humanists.'

the course of this programme humanists may find new lines of cleavage determined by real issues and conflicts of value. Popular humanism may shrug off the old and fail to see the new, but a full-blooded humanist though willing to accept the test of practice is bound to consider the full range of human interests in the light of experience. Popular humanism is valid and necessary, and it could be a good thing if it gained ground and made irresistible demands. Perhaps, however, it is creative in opposition, dangerous in power.

Fall of the Pillars

Dr Gerhard Szczesny of West Germany, in a book which has been widely discussed on the Continent, *The Future of Un-belief*, speaks dramatically of God, immortality and freewill as 'the three pillars of unreason'. Dramatically, because not so long ago these were the three pillars of reason, the axiomatic tenets of the religion of reason, which was universal if not yet world-wide. The collapse of these pillars erected by reason and demolished by reason is generally accepted by Protestant theologians, most of whom have abandoned natural theology as the ground of Christian faith. Christian Revelation has to stand on its own without support from axioms of reason. The drama might be taken out of this reversal by suggesting that there have been and are rational and irrational ideas of God, immortality and freewill. If the collapse of the pillars merely means the translation into mythology of the Old Man in the Sky and the free and immortal spirit independent of the body and destined to everlasting bliss or punishment (even though it be a judgement by good deeds and not by correct beliefs), then most theologians are going to say that at last people are beginning to catch up with them and not to worry that myths are myths. Therefore one may well ask if humanism and the traditional beliefs of religion are not opposed merely as crude affirmations and denials which no instructed person could want to make today. This is indeed how some people do see it.

The answer is simple and short, and has already been given: if there are humanists in the sense of this chapter who want to call themselves Christians and practise Christianity, that is *their* humanism. There are some, but they are exceptional and likely to remain few. And the difference between humanists and the rest is likely to remain practically important. For humanists are not preoccupied with the re-erection of these pillars, nor concerned with that kind of operation in any way at all. Having made assumptions which dispose of that and turn them away from that, they are turned wholly towards the human development for which they have taken on responsibility, animated solely by the sentiments and interests which bind them to the concrete world. From beginning to end, humanism has these three roots. Or call them pillars.

A Starting-point

This first chapter is headed 'preliminaries' and the first sentence plunges straight in. But humanism itself is a preliminary, a beginning in common which is completed each for himself in the personal life of the humanist. Therefore these preliminary indications of what humanism is and is not and what it can and cannot do are intended to warn against mistaken expectations. Humanism is not a fully fledged philosophy, like Sinbad's roc to whose leg the neophyte humanist can bind himself securely and be borne into the empyrean. Its virtue is its modesty, its having no magic; its value is its realism, its instruction in dependence only on the dependable. Humanism helps no one who is not helping himself and cannot be persuaded to do so.

A voice of complaint says: 'I have made the bleak assumptions because I must and I have taken on this onerous responsibility for myself and for mankind on the strength only of my own response to the world. You call this "humanism" but that is only your gimmicky word for my blood, sweat and tears. The assumption–responsibility–response which you have called the three pillars of humanism give no more support than the tallies pegged in the seed plots of an agronomist; they are no more than your labels for what I find I must do and am doing.'

The complaint is not to be answered: humanism *is* a description before it is a prescription; its spontaneity is its veracity. But the spontaneous beginning can be cultivated and developed. To have identified and established as a norm a spontaneous way of taking and tackling the world is already an advance and an encouragement which leads on to further advance and encouragement, with the result that more people are enabled to live to better purpose, to use and develop resources within themselves and available to them, to find others to whom they can speak, whom they can help, and by whom they can be helped, and to gain a perspective of their own lives and of the life of mankind. The following chapters will try to show how this claim is made good.

2

THE OPEN MIND

Nature is her own standard, one thing throws light on another.
Epicurus

. . . in his own breast does not every man carry about with him a possible Socrates, in that power of a disinterested play of consciousness upon his stock notions and habits, of which this wise and admirable man gave all through his lifetime the great example, and which was the secret of his incomparable influence?
Matthew Arnold

An Ambiguous Phrase

ASSUMPTION – responsibility – response: these three natural roots of humanism involve the three sides of human nature usually spoken of as intellect, will and feeling. All three sides are equally important to humanists as to others. But the humanist is a rationalist, one who puts reason first; and he stresses the open mind, dedication to a disinterested search for truth. There seem to be contradictions here if humanism is a concern for balanced development and if humanism begins with two massive assumptions which close the mind and put a dogmatic end to the disinterested search for truth.

The cult of an open mind and talk of a disinterested quest for truth is usually cant, and invites a good spit. However, two things have to be said in justification of this way of speaking. The open mind is an empty mind if it never makes up its mind. This cannot be what is meant. Second, although it would be absurd to think of humanists as engaged night and day (or even on Tuesdays and Thursdays) in a disinterested pursuit of truth, care for truth as a primary value is a distinguishing characteristic of humanists. They want to know first on what ground they can dig dependable foundations and build their house. When they have taken considerable trouble to do this, they are like other people; they have a vested interest, and do not want to have to evacuate or demolish their home. However, they are not worse than others at seeing that this may be necessary and recognizing when it has become necessary. They ought to be much better at this than others, and perhaps most of them really are.

The faith of the humanist is first of all in reason, in the reliability of tested evidence. There are some matters in which the head is sovereign, some in which the heart is queen. When Pascal says, 'The heart has its reasons of which reason knows nothing', he is commending trust in the heart rather than the head on some matters. There are matters of choice on which the heart is entitled to have the main say, but the choice of life is certainly not one of them – in the humanist's view. If the humanist did have a religious faith, he would hold it conditionally on rational grounds, retaining his primary faith in reason. In the days of natural religion, in the eighteenth century, this was done. With the subsequent erosion of the foundations of natural theology this position has collapsed. The three pillars of reason have become pillars of unreason. A resort to the reasons of the heart which the mind does not comprehend looks tricky. An open mind means a candour to which trickery is repugnant. It means exposure, not covering up the vulnerable places. An open mind is vulnerable to evidence.

By comparison a religious faith may not be vulnerable. If the believer will not allow that any experience could falsify his belief, he does not have an open mind about it because it is not founded on rational grounds. His faith is trust in something other than the reliability of tested evidence. This trust is likely to be in God, who is then at once the author and the object of the faith. The believer will regard the unbeliever in this case not as deficient in rational understanding but as defective in will: he is proud, stubborn, self-sufficient and wilful; he cannot believe because he will not let himself believe. The evidence may be insufficient by the canons of reason, but if the inquirer were open-hearted and truly open-minded, if he would acknowledge his dependence instead of fortifying himself in his independence, his hard-headed and hard-hearted stiff-necked resistance would be softened and he would experience trust and enter into the life of grace. Thus the believer accuses the rationalist, and therewith the humanist, of being closed to a certain possibility which he will not entertain because it threatens to take away the independent ground of his being.* The believer goes on to use reason against reason, deploying rational argument to show the limited competence of reason and the irrationality of arguments against religious faith. Reason may not require faith, but it does allow faith.

Rationalist and believer, then, accuse each other of being closed and invulnerable where each should be open and exposed. The one is closed to the relevance of empirical evidence, the other to the possibility of a divine dispensation not contrary to reason because beyond the scope of reason. The humanist is a rationalist. He feels that all is lost if he lets go his faith in reason. This is his choice; he is anchored in reason and he navigates by reason. His beliefs are vulnerable to empirical evidence, and this he accepts. The rational ground of his beliefs as the ultimate ground of belief is also open to criticism. The Christian invites him to abandon rationality as his ultimate ground, to recognize the subordinate role and

---

*The Christian idea of the humanist as unwilling to believe because resolved to stand on his own is well represented by the speech which Milton puts into the mouth of Mammon:

> Let us not then pursue
> By force impossible, by leave obtain'd
> Unacceptable, though in Heav'n, our state
> Of splendid vassalage, but rather seek
> Our good from our own selves, and from our own
> Live to our selves, though in this vast recess,
> Free, and to none accountable, preferring
> Hard liberty before the easie yoke
> Of servile Pomp. Our greatness will appear
> Then most conspicuous, when great things of small,
> Useful of hurtful, prosperous of adverse
> We can create, and in what place so e're
> Thrive under evil, and work ease out of pain
> Through labour and endurance.
>
> *Paradise Lost* bk ii, ll. 249–62

limited scope of reason and the total dependence of the human condition, to repent not argue, and to trust. The humanist rejects this invitation, but if he is to remain open-minded he does not dismiss it once for all; he knows that it stands, that it is conceivable he may change his mind, not because of further evidence, but because of a change of heart and a change of ground.

Truth and Reason

Reason is the final standard for the humanist, but nobody in practice can live all the time with complete intellectual austerity. Christians have their ideal in holiness, cleansing of the will in absolute obedience to God. Is intellectual rigour the comparable ideal of humanists, since they base themselves on reason? A Victorian rationalist, W. K. Clifford, said: 'It is wrong always, everywhere, and for anyone, to believe anything upon insufficient evidence.' By this standard every humanist is guilty, as every Christian by the standard of holiness. But perfect rationality is not like holiness a total ideal. There is more than reason in the life of reason or it is not reasonable.

One ambiguity has been removed. The open mind is not vacant and unfurnished. Ideally, it is furnished only with beliefs held on sufficient evidence and remains open to the changes required by further evidence. There is still ambiguity about 'the quest for truth'. Perhaps 'truth' is never used without the definite article in this phrase unless the notion in mind is 'Truth', an absolute or transcendental truth which is different in kind from the truth of propositions which are either true or false. Rationalists do not use the word 'truth' in this sense. They use it strictly with reference to a proposition conveying information which can be checked. This is not the kind of truth that makes men free, perhaps, although enlightenment is linked with emancipation. The truth of propositions is not a truth about the world as a whole, nor a truth that is beyond the world; it is simply the establishment of attested facts of a definite and limited kind. To be engaged in the pursuit of truth in this modest sense is to be a scientist at work in some field of empirical investigation, piecing together what goes with what and what follows what in the phenomena studied. Therefore only those humanists who happen to be scientists are engaged in a disinterested search for truth, and any one of these is likely to be employed on some speciality far removed from the centre of human interests. Clearly, to say that humanists care for truth as their first priority cannot mean that every one of them is professionally engaged in some branch of science, and puts his professional business first in his life. What, then, does it mean, if anything?

A full answer would have to be a long one. Briefly it means that humanists want to know the truth about the human situation before they decide how to live, and that they depend for this knowledge exclusively, in the long run, on propositions of the kind which scientists are engaged in establishing and which remain open to question and to public checks.

This assumption that only empirical natural knowledge is the truth is sometimes called 'positivism', and it is useful to have a name for it. But to say that humanism on the intellectual side is positivism might be misleading. Any name here is a trap because it suggests a particular disputable theory of knowledge. Science does not dispose of the 'problem of knowledge': science is the problem of knowledge. In taking science as the definition of knowledge humanists are making two practical assumptions based on the experience of some two thousand years of cultural tradition, not espousing a particular philosophical theory of knowledge. The two general assumptions are: 1. there is no absolute knowledge which is beyond question, neither within the mind nor outside in any tradition; 2. the criteria and procedures of the empirical sciences provide the most reliable way of trying to resolve questions of fact and establish by agreement what the facts are.

If 'truth' and 'knowledge' are 'science', what is 'reason'? Pope in the eighteenth century called reason 'the god within the mind'. The phrase well represents the notion of reason as the godlike essence of man, akin to the divine mind that framed the universe, which is therefore able to decipher and spell out what is there, to 'think the thoughts of God'. As this universal faculty, reason was assumed to be embodied in certain innate ideas independent of experience which were directly known to be necessarily true and the foundation of all reliable knowledge. The law within corresponded to the law without, issuing from a common Author. This doctrine is perhaps not held by anybody today in the same form. But its descendants are among us in contemporary clothes. In contrast with this notion of reason as an inborn faculty in every man is the notion of reason as embodied in certain procedures of 'reasoning', the methods of the sciences, a cultural discovery which has been elaborated and established as a tradition. Whatever biological predispositions or adaptive responses there are in the human animal, necessary to a complete account of 'reason', the learned methods, the cultural tools, make reason progressive and reliable. From language itself to laboratories, reason has a history and is not a metaphysical absolute of any kind. It is a possession of some societies, rather than of man. Its universality is not yet.

The rationalism of the humanist is therefore a reliance on science, a cooperative and publicly controlled thinking, rather than on 'my reason' which tells me what 'stands to reason'. However, there are some real doubts and difficulties here: 1. science is not all that certain; 2. many of my opinions and a good deal of the information I make use of daily hardly can be 'scientific'; 3. science does not tell me what to choose nor how to live; 4. science does not tell me about the world as a whole, does not answer 'first and last questions', does not deal with religious nor metaphysical issues.

Public and Private Aspects of Rationality

Science easily becomes the new superstition. The outsider sees its miracles and gives it his faith and worship. Or he gets a glimpse of the inside and sees almost as many sects and rival doctrines as in the old religion. Science is only human. All the same, the human failings which mar every human enterprise have here, as they have in democratic politics, certain built-in correctives. There is a climate of exposure, a standing incentive to challenge and try to prove false established results. And the tests are demonstrable, and repeatable, appeals to experience, not success in verbal plausibility. The scientific tradition is an inestimable cultural achievement which can be depreciated and destroyed, again like democracy. The tradition, and it is a sensitive highly organized one, is in the hands of the scientists, but it is also in the hands of the public. Superstitious veneration or ignorant 'science' fantasy and cynical depreciation ('statistics prove anything') contribute equally to making a climate in which science could not flourish. Humanists, as the 'party' for science, have to try to form a model public opinion in this respect, based on a proper understanding of the nature, the uses and the limits of science. Science is not the bible of the humanists by any means, but in one respect there is a parallel: a professed Christian for whom the Bible was a closed book could not be taken very seriously. 'Numeracy' like literacy is an elementary qualification, a qualification for citizenship.

In a strict sense the opinions one holds and expresses and the information one uses in everyday life are not scientific. They hardly ever have the precise and limited meaning and application which distinguish scientific propositions. Although it would not be feasible to carry into everyday life the methods and rigour of the natural sciences, (it would be absurd to try), there are rational standards of responsibility which do apply to the opinions one holds and expresses and the information on which one relies. Reading the correspondence of John Stuart Mill, one is impressed by the strenuous work which went to the making of his opinions and by the firm and full account he could always give of them. Anyone would be driven from society who asked of every statement: what does it mean? is it true? what use is going to be made of it? But too few of us too seldom do ask such questions even in our own minds of the statements we listen to, or which we hear ourselves making. The bracing effect of introducing them more frequently and not too formally might bring home how flabby, feeble and tedious most talk is.

Responsibility of course begins with one's own opinions, but it does not end there, for a high private standard is not good enough in matters of public concern where we have all to maintain the standard or there is none. To maintain rational standards in the expression, reception and propagation of opinions, however, is not the whole of responsibility in verbal conduct of this kind. When young I got into sad disfavour for making a critical examination of what a person said, as though it were a disembodied statement, or indeed a dead body for dissection and learning. I did learn. I learned that total disregard of the author of a statement in preoccupation with the merits of the statement, however admirably impartial, was not a happy way of conducting intellectual business. In sum, rationality is not enough, even when what is in question is the validity of an opinion or the adequacy and accuracy of certain information. Opinions are sensitive parts of people, even if they are merely borrowed, perhaps most of all in that case. Opinions are not all one's own work; there is a current public stamp on some, and they are currently in the intellectual trade going on, and can buy esteem. Standards are established when only earned opinions are accepted in exchange for esteem. Half quitting metaphors, obviously there ought to be a rational standard in the opinion market, and obviously this market is a sensitive social nexus in which people demand and observe the standard or there is none. If there is none the opinionated and the inert have it all their own way, and the others withdraw to their own circles.

Responsible opinions are matched by responsible decisions. A responsibly taken decision involves more of the person and is more formative than a responsibly held opinion, although indeed opinions are inert unless they influence decisions. A decision responsibly taken is a decision taken by rational standards, but it is more personal than an opinion need be, less 'scientific'. This will be discussed more fully in the next section. All that need be said here is that there is a proper way to reach an 'informed' decision, and this procedure is the rational standard. In so far as it is not wholly and solely a question of what the facts are, if a decision is required in the light of the facts, then this is likely to involve considerations and commitments which have a personal character and weight, and the decision though personal may be rational but cannot be 'scientific'.

Some opinions may be lightly held and some decisions spontaneously taken. Sometimes a thorough job is required. Seriously to make up one's mind is to reopen one's mind, to question again in this new context the assumptions and principles one has accepted. To take a decisive step is to reopen the personality, to reconsider settled motives, aims, purposes, ideals: what one is. This is not everyday work, nor perhaps a healthy nightly habit. In the days of piety Christians kept spiritual diaries in which at the end of the day they recorded lapses and progress in the life of grace and meditated on Providence and their own behaviour. This does not make pleasant reading, and would hardly be improved if the life of reason instead of the life of grace were made the occasion of such self-examination. All the same, self-examination there must be if standards of rationality are to be maintained in opinions and decisions. Rather than by the clock or the calendar, the occasions for this are to be determined by the actual times when opinions are being formed or decisions taken. In this actuality self-examination has a formative influence it does not have in routine.

Reason as Servant

What now is the relevance of science or rational procedures to the choice of values? Some philosophers would seem to say, none. David Hume in the eighteenth century was one of the first to call attention to the logical point that a proposition which states what ought to be cannot be inferred from a proposition which states what is the case. Value cannot be logically derived from fact. How, then, are judgements of value and judgements of fact to be related? 'Reason is and ought only to be', said Hume, 'the slave of the passions.' In our century, Bertrand Russell has explicitly reaffirmed this dictum: 'It expresses a view to which I, like every man who attempts to be reasonable, fully subscribe. "Reason" has a perfectly clear and precise meaning. It signifies the choice of the right means to an end that you wish to achieve. It has nothing to do with the choice of ends.'

Here are two eminent and highly respected philosophers who are exemplary humanists committing themselves unreservedly to an extreme position on a point of fundamental importance to humanists as rationalists. They are plainly wrong if what they say is taken literally. If Hume had said, 'Reason is and ought only to be the civil servant of the passions', the relationship would have been better expressed, but he could hardly be expected to have anticipated the working of the administration in the twentieth century. As to Russell, reason, that is to say attested information, has almost everything to do with the choice of ends, and of values.

I do not *have* to choose, prefer, desire something because of what it is, but if I *do* prefer, desire, choose something it is because of what it is. If I believe that God exists I do not have to live in obedience to him, but if I do believe that he is creator and sustainer of all that is or can be, that is justification enough for my total obedience. Judgements of fact are far more relevant to and intimately related with judgements of value than is indicated by the relation of means to independently chosen ends. Choice is logically dependent upon knowledge (established by reasoning from experience) although it does not follow logically from knowledge as a necessary inference. I choose something which I know (am informed about), I choose it by comparison with alternatives about which I am also informed, and I choose it in the light of what my choice will involve as far as my best judgement can determine. This choice of ends or values by making comparisons and bringing in relevant 'considerations', of which a rational account can be given, is certainly different from a 'blind' passion which wants to know only how to get hold of the object which it would seize. This passion stays neither to know the object nor to consider the probable consequences of seizing it, and does not consider and compare any possible alternative object. Actually, not even animals behave in this

36

way. The tiger does not spring precipitately, for fear of losing the prey. The arctic wolf does not select for attack the fat and healthy caribou, but the poor and sickly one. Delaying the spring, the tiger adopts what experience shows to be the appropriate means for the end in view. Similarly, it can be argued that the wolf follows what has proved to be the best method for satisying hunger reliably with a tolerable expenditure of energy. But in the latter case there is effective choice of ends, a rudimentary comparison of values. If the notion of 'end' is restricted to those ultimate ends like the satisfaction of hunger which are simply given and which reason can neither choose nor refuse, this is an arbitrary restriction that confuses discussion. To say that reason 'has nothing to do with the choice of ends' is silly if the ends are such that they are given and cannot be chosen. If they can be chosen, it is a contradiction in terms because 'choice' means getting information and making comparisons with possible alternatives, if the end is to be indeed fully chosen. What we want has to be learned, just as much as how to get it.

Reason is not in competition with the 'passions', and there is no struggle for mastery at all. The part of reason is simply to organize and to inform the choice, whether of means or of ends. Deliberative choice is a rational process. To make a pause, to formulate possible alternatives, to bring together the relevant information and considerations, and to put feelings and desires into this context is not to put 'reason' and the 'passions' into any juxtaposition. Rather, one might regard only the procedure as rational, and all the factors that are brought together as equally non-rational.

How, then, is the choice determined? Suppose the 'passions' are overruled by such 'considerations' as public opinion or 'the findings of experience', are they not subdued by reason? 'Overruled' here of course is not an intervention from outside; the person overrules his own passions in deference to public opinion or to the wisdom of the race. This is his own choice, expressing what in the circumstances of the case he most cares about. A choice is not an impersonal calculation, nor a chemical reaction.

All the same, there is room for uneasiness here. To return to Hume: 'The liveliest thought is inferior to the dullest sensation.' This may be dismissed as 'patently absurd', but it recalls the remark of Keats: 'O, for a life of sensations rather than of thoughts.' The enmity of thought and life may not be necessary, but it is to be feared. Reason is the steward of our inherited estate, and we have to be careful not to allow ourselves to be swindled out of our birthright of spontaneous life. This is the priceless inheritance which it is for reason to cultivate and develop and make productive, not take over. The 'passions' are the most personal part of us and the best that is in us (also the worst). The person who chooses and decides, in doing so chooses and decides himself. He identifies himself with some of his own passions and their corresponding aspirations and ideals, and establishes and develops in himself a life of his own vigorous enough to seek and to use information and to give to other interests the consideration that is due. If this is all that is meant, 'Reason is and ought only to be the slave of the passions.' But, slave or parasite, these are misleading metaphors unless taken as warnings of dangerous liabilities, not as true likenesses. At best, reason is the tutor that brings on our spontaneous life through learning to its consummation in a self-creating personality.

The Scientific Picture

The humanist relies on the empirical sciences for his world-picture, which then completely takes the place of the mythological world-picture which comes down with religious tradition. There are, however, three major difficulties in taking a world-view from the empirical sciences: no scientist is engaged in producing one; science is a sieve with a rather coarse mesh through which there may pass a good deal that is of the highest importance; science does not undertake to ask nor answer 'first and last questions' of the kind with which metaphysicians and theologians have been concerned. In other words, science has serious limits, and recognition and acceptance of these limits may leave scope for legitimate non-scientific rational efforts to understand the world.

No scientist is engaged in producing the scientific world-picture, each is engaged in making a more or less small contribution to a more or less small part of the picture. Whether or not a world-picture can be eventually built up on positivist lines as an overall result of the work of all the empirical sciences is itself a question, a question for the philosopher – if he is interested. What, anyhow, is really meant by a scientific world-picture? The ordinary educated person has some idea of the stellar universe, of the evolution of species, of the chemical basis of life, and in general of the map of knowledge. The map may be sketchy and woefully inadequate and inaccurate in many parts, in these respects not unlike an ordinary educated person's idea of the geographical map. But most of the regions are there in name and position, and more detailed knowledge can be filled in if wanted, and when wanted the specialist will be consulted rather than the philosopher or the scientific journalist. So that the world-picture, if it means anything, means something else. In the history of thinking it has meant a comprehensive hypothesis, a dominant pattern or type of order or structure or process which unifies all that is. This is something more or other than a synopsis or synthesis of the sciences. There is a field here for rational exploration and speculation open to the philosopher, and to the interested layman who follows him. Before dealing further with this limitation of science under 'first and last questions', a word about the second major difficulty, the coarse scientific mesh.

In particular, what bothers people is that personality slips through. If the human sciences can study only manifest behaviour, the man within as one knows him in oneself escapes. Multiple descriptions may accumulate more and more data, but the living uniqueness of the person is not susceptible of analysis. Is this mere prejudice unworthy of a rationalist, a surviving remnant of the old notion of man as godlike in essence? Or is there something here which science cannot reach but which is important all the same?

The answer is that the unique person is indeed something

which science cannot reach. But then science does not pretend to do so. Nor does science deal with more lowly organisms as individuals, nor even with atoms, nor the smallest particles. Science works with generalities and abstractions, not with concrete individuals. The general laws of the sciences apply to individuals, but not exhaustively. How they apply, indeed whether they apply, has to be observed and is not more than a prediction of probability. Physical particles and lowly organisms are on the whole simpler and more regular in their behaviour than human beings, and the differences of individuals can therefore be more safely ignored and the behaviour of all more reliably predicted. But the difference is only one of degree. Persons are subject to science and exempt from science precisely in the same way as toads or microbes, but most of them have more possibilities. Science selects and simplifies in order to be science, and in the case of men and women more is left out that can make a difference than in the case of simpler organisms. Man is not a god who is too subtle to be held by rational categories, but neither is he merely an animal, for nothing is. 'Animal' is an abstraction, a class name; it has no specific character, no horns, no tail, and does not exist. Man as a species is all that he is found to be in a full experience of him down the ages. The sciences make a rich contribution to that understanding, but so do the works of man which belong to his entire history, the arts, religions, institutions and cultures in which he has expressed and objectified himself. The richest concept of man, informed by a deep study of his behaviour in different times and places as recorded or objectified in his works, does not in any way take the place of, nor supersede, nor render otiose the particular person whom one encounters. One's perception of him can be informed by this concept, but not anticipated. Moreover, most encounters with individual persons are not for the sake of accumulating data for a general knowledge of man.

Science, then, is indeed a coarse mesh through which the most valuable things pass, if it is supposed that science is a filtering or fishing operation, which it is not. Rather, science is a map which enables us to find our way about and explore and enjoy places for ourselves without getting lost. Only when one gives up going out and sits at home with the map, when science becomes a substitute for life, is there the kind of reduction which is sometimes called 'scientism', an abuse of science which the humanist can only abhor, for it spells 'life for the sake of science'.

First and Last Questions

Questions about the nature of existence and the destiny of man, how things began and how they will end, why there is something rather than nothing, and why what is is as it is, are not questions which any of the sciences asks and are not questions which any of the sciences could attempt to answer. This kind of question is not one which the sciences are unable to answer at present but can hope with the development of knowledge to be in a position to answer at some time. They are outside the terms of reference of the positive sciences.

There are at least three alternatives. The positivist Auguste Comte said that he was not an atheist because that was to take theology seriously. Metaphysical questions may be ignored as unreal and not serious. Or they may be accepted as legitimate questions, perhaps indeed as the most poignant questions for a human being, without any belief that they can be resolved. Or whilst it is accepted that such questions cannot be answered by empirical propositions such as are established by the sciences, it may be held that 'answers' can be found in some 'revelation' or in some form of extra-sensory experience, some experience of the Transcendent. Which, if any, of these alternatives does the humanist take? Paul Tillich has said of the empirical attitude of positivism that it is either a humble acknowledgement of man's finitude or arrogant dismissal of the concern for ultimate truth. Is the humanist humble or arrogant, a 'reverent agnostic' or an agnostic of Comte's stamp, contemptuous of the very questions because they are not questions he can hope to answer?

Before one falls for this division into arrogant and humble agnostics, tough minds and tender spirits, the questions at issue should be examined to see whether or not they are legitimate and deserve to be taken seriously. Is 'concern for ultimate truth' a preoccupation with an ultimate Why? which science does not raise and cannot answer? If so, is there any sense in it, since the only answers to Why? are reasons such as causes of the kind science can trace or purposes of the kind with which all human beings are familiar? Such reasons can never produce a FIRST CAUSE nor a FINAL PURPOSE. And to suppose that there must be unknowable absolutes of this kind seems to be gratuitous. Perhaps, however, this is to intellectualize 'the concern for ultimate truth'. Perhaps 'a humble acknowledgement of man's finitude' means a sense of infinite dependence upon one knows not what. Again, man is finitely dependent upon nature, men are interdependent, and the individual person has his own independence. Respect for these conditions of human existence keeps men within the bounds of all due modesty.

The ultimate questions ultimately persist, however; they haunt the human mind and will not be laid, whatever formulas are pronounced. There is a stubborn refusal to accept the world as self-explanatory and self-justifying. Yet all things are equally explicable and inexplicable: explicable in that it can in principle be shown how everything came about or can be brought about and how it is related to other things; inexplicable in that everything is equally 'given' as it is and has to be accepted as it is without further question. Our thinking begins and ends with acceptance of things as we find them. Our thinking is done wholly in terms of what we find; one thing throws light on another; we make comparisons; we use metaphors and analogies. The proper modesty of our thinking is this ultimate acceptance of what is as the standard of what is. To impose, or look for, standards drawn from our own aspirations is the sublime arrogance, if it is arrogance one fears – or if one wants to accuse the other side.

Beyond positivism, there is legitimate metaphysical inquiry, however. An inquiry into the kind of order there is in the universe, and whether indeed it is a universe, is a different kind of inquiry from that raised by 'first and last questions', and although conclusive answers have not been reached and may not be attainable, some progress may be made by reviewing the history of thought and classifying the types of theory and assessing their virtues and inadequacies. Some men will always want to engage in speculations of this kind, and so long as the argument is rationally conducted it is congruent with positivism and the philosophy of science.

Some humanists who are not philosophers crave the stimulus and the imaginative grip on the world which they feel a metaphysic gives them. The Idealist philosophers now in eclipse satisfied this craving abundantly. The legendary popularity of Teilhard de Chardin indicates the strength of the craving. There is no humanist metaphysic, but any humanist who shivers or feels ashamed has a choice of outfit off the peg.

Again, it may be said that to oust theology with metaphysics is to intellectualize the question. God, after all, is not an hypothesis but the supreme object, not primarily an explanation but source and goal – and all else. The sheer inexplicability of the world in which we find ourselves, it may be thought, makes it the more awful and should drive us to respond with a sense of infinite dependence. The humanist remains on his feet. He is not a 'reverent agnostic', chiefly because his acceptance of the 'given' is ambivalent. This ambivalence is tolerable only because it is impersonal, not love–hate but enjoyment–endurance, and because people can be helped to have less to endure and more to enjoy. Enjoyment–endurance is the link with all mankind which involves our sympathies, affections and imagination, and by that hold involves us in the moral task of improving conditions. Beyond the lot and life of mankind is the natural world which brings what Wordsworth called 'the consolation of images', and the essential kinship which Keats called 'a fellowship with essences'. Not worship, but a total participation in the life of the world is the humanist's aspiration. For humanism is not religion but it is more than 'morals without religion', or it beggars the unbeliever.

Truth, then, is put first and reason is relied on to attain and attest it. But 'the open mind' is not a cant phrase for a disinterested pursuit of truth in which nobody is seriously engaged except perhaps the professional scientist, for it means a general openness to further experience and to the experience of others, which includes a reopening of personality in every important act of choice or decision and a continuous growth through learning. In this context, the open mind is the growing-point of a self-creating person.

3

THE OPEN SOCIETY

Men . . . cannot change their natures. All they can do
is to change their situations.
                                          David Hume

Are we not, then, with this gigantic intention of ours of
smoothing down every sharp edge and corner in life,
utilizing the best means of turning mankind into sand!
Small, soft, round, infinite sand!
                                          Friedrich Nietzsche

Public Means to Private Ends

'RESEARCH' is the key word in modern culture. Post-graduate study for a higher university degree is mainly a training in the methods and standards of research; as a by-product, thousands of accepted theses are annually housed and catalogued in university libraries as contributions to knowledge available to students. Research in the sciences and in scholarship is the same the world over in all essential procedures and by this means knowledge is methodically expanded and made public. Although there is general agreement about the procedures of research and about the knowledge thereby established, there may be wide differences in the interpretations of basic knowledge, in the uses that are made of it, and in the fields of research financed and developed. A society may devote a high proportion of its resources to military technology and space exploration. Just conceivably, another society that disposes of equivalent resources may devote as high a proportion to medical and social research. Roman Catholics, Protestants, Muslims, and Marxist–Leninists may engage in research or accept the results of research, but they are likely to make different interpretations of the results, to use them for different purposes, and to favour or pursue different lines of research.

Modern culture, then, as turning on research, is open in two decisive ways: the methods and the findings of research are public, open to challenge from any quarter; and the results of research are open to different interpretations and uses. There is a basic agreement (about procedures and findings) supporting wide differences in purpose and use. This pattern of public methods furnishing possibilities for private choice is a key pattern in modern social order. 'Private' choice may range from an individual person to a whole nation or any substantial group. A society that depends on research is bound to be open in the first sense, since tampering with the procedures or the findings of research is certain to destroy it in the end as a resource. But in the second sense a society that does employ and profit by research may be closed if the authorities restrict research to certain fields, or restrict the use of its results, or adopt and adapt them within a set ideological framework.

Comparable to these agreed procedures in research for reaching agreement about what the facts are there are procedures for reaching agreement in practice about what shall be done. These procedures are less exact (and less widely accepted and practised) because 'interests' are directly involved (what people want) as well as 'information'. There seems to be more justification for not accepting the procedures for reaching agreement in practice than there can be for rejecting the procedures of research – which would be merely stupid. By democratic procedure a simple majority may decide what is to be done. If what is decided in this way affects my interests adversely, I shall have real difficulty in accepting the result as guaranteed by the procedure in the same way in which the results of a piece of research are warranted by the procedures followed. Thus it may seem that there is no real comparison between the scientific procedures of research and the procedures of political democracy. They certainly do not enjoy the same universality, and they do not appear to have the same force.

All the same, they are fully comparable in being attempts to control and develop public experience in a rational way. The knowledge established by research is the most reliable to be obtained. There is no alternative as good. Similarly, the alternatives to democratic procedures are likely to bring greater disadvantages to more people. For if authority is wielded by an arbitrary few, however well qualified, they are more than likely (on the evidence of experience) to legislate and act in their own interests. In any case there is no incentive, no sanction, to bring their own interest into line with the general interest. The basis of power and government has to be an army, a police, a class, a party, the people. Rule by a party or a coalition representing a majority and answerable to an electorate based on a universal adult franchise is an historically established procedure that has proved more serviceable to the interests of more people than any alternative device.

The knowledge established by research is public and subject to checks, and is progressive in that it raises questions that lead on to further knowledge. Similarly, the laws and policies established by democratic procedures are open to revision, and indeed reversal, in the light of the experience which they have created. A democratic decision expressed in a statute or in a public policy is the most rational and responsible political decision possible, to the extent that the interests affected are adequately consulted and the information relied on is the fullest and soundest available. Modern techniques of communication and of collecting and organizing information should improve the standard of rationality in taking account of relevant information and of responsibility in considering affected interests.

Not only are decisions taken in this way the most rational in the sense of being most fully 'informed', they also have a moral authority, comparable to the intellectual authority of a scientific judgement, which no public decision taken in any other way can have. For the interests affected by the decisions are party to the decisions, in the sense that they have made their representations (or have been free to do so) and have assented to the procedures which provide for the appointment and recall of the competent decision-making authority. To refuse to comply with decisions taken in this way is to be ungovernable, that is to say anti-social and basically immoral. In exceptional cases of conscience when one chooses to be a law unto oneself, an outlaw, one may have to do this and to suffer the consequences. But the essence of such cases is that they are exceptional, and rarely justifiable. Legislation and policy arrived at by democratic procedures are morally agreed, as knowledge established by scientific procedures is intellectually agreed.

In these ways, democratic political procedures and institutions are comparable and complementary to scientific cultural procedures and institutions. Both are rationally grounded in repeated experience. Both are themselves provisional, open to further experience, and establish provisional knowledge or provisional laws and policies, open to revision in the light of further experience or new situations. Both are in this sense self-correcting and 'progressive'. Both are public procedures of which the results may be used for private purposes, since laws and policies, like knowledge, create and limit possibilities open to choice. They are complementary because democratic decisions are greatly facilitated by and depend on reliable public information, and because in a modern society the fields of research which are developed and the use that is made of results are largely a social responsibility in which all affected interests should have their share, leaving room also for the private development of fields which do not attract public funds.

Both these systems of procedure, then, are in effect agreed rules for establishing provisional agreement (knowledge, laws) which is the most dependable obtainable because it is kept open to revision by agreed rules. The 'open' society is a society founded mainly on these two systems of rules, and therefore based on certain forms of agreement and striving for fuller agreement. Just because it is firmly founded on public agreement kept systematically open to disagreement and revision, the open society can afford private disagreement in the form of a wide and extending range of choice, facilitated and regulated by the public procedures. The open society is open in these two ways. It provides public means to diverse private ends, and the public means (knowledge or information, laws or policies) are open to improvement by public means. These two classical systems of rules or procedures, science and politics, which define an open society are fairly sophisticated and historically late, but they represent the rational development of human society.

The Social Basis of Man and the Moral Basis of Society

Man is not born human, he becomes human in a society. If a human infant survives outside the care of other human beings, he remains for a time potentially human and then possibly becomes incapable of development as a human being. The child brought up by wolves becomes neither wolf nor man. That man is the product of culture and becomes specifically human in a particular culture is the first truth about man. To recognize this is to accept a basic relativity in the existence and nature of man. The belief of eighteenth-century humanists that 'men are in every respect what the laws make them to be' is only an exaggeration of a truth. Where then is the uniqueness and universality that constitute the dignity of being human? Solely in the potentiality of human self-determination and in the potentiality of personal self-determination. 'Man is the future of man' when historical development has gone far enough to enable men to overrule fate and edge their destiny towards a destination. Man becomes a person when he is able to choose and make himself because he finds alternatives. Otherwise, human existence remains closely linked with animal existence.

The age-old alternative to this evolutionary view has been that man is divinely endowed with an immortal essence. The truth about man is neither this nor his lack of any intrinsic character which endows him with highness. But this endowment is a potentiality, certain possibilities and the responsibility for their development. The permanent truth in the religious myths of man is the recognition of his nature and destiny in terms of possibility and responsibility. Man is the only animal that is saved or damned. One may say that he has three natures: biological, cultural, personal. Today, within biological limits, he has increasing cultural resources to choose

49

and to become what he would be. What *he* would be: the meaning of an open society is that this representative *he* shall not stand for the human race nor for any social choice, imposed and induced, but for personal choices socially supported and endowed.

Man, then, is born potentially human and becomes human in a society; he is bred in a culture. In so far as he never knows anything that is not mediated through that culture he remains imprisoned within it, relativized by it. When he becomes aware of other cultures, other ways of being human, he can begin to separate himself from the culture in which he is bred and to identify himself as man. This independence, though of supreme importance, is relative, for man remains always dependent upon society and largely determined by the culture in which he is bred. Nevertheless, the relative personal independence which he can achieve is the supreme human achievement.

Therefore the societies that support personal independence and the cultures that breed it are the most distinctively human. Most early societies have a politico-religious basis. Religious institutions, practices and beliefs are in common and create and regulate a social order which has tremendous sanctions divine and human. When the institutions lose their hold in common acceptance and the practices decline and the beliefs are radically put in question by many, religion, without ceasing to be of first importance to many, becomes impracticable as the basis of society. There is a shift, over the years and possibly without any dramatic moment, to a 'secular' basis. This new basis is politico-moral. What men and women are united upon has ceased to be religious practices and beliefs about the nature of existence and the conduct of personal life, and has become agreement upon the rules for living and working together. The fundamental agreement is about the rules regulating politics, governing access to and the responsible exercise of power. Upon this basis there are rules of many different kinds, from the rules of debate to rules of the road, from manners to morals, from civil rights to company law, from statutes to judicial procedures. Rules of all kinds provide the modern basis for living and working together in a shared society. Mere rules, however, give only a politico-technical coherence to social cooperation and leave it lacking the social identity and continuity, the human warmth and contact, the binding sanctions, the shared public life of a great religious tradition as the basis of a whole society. When the Roman Church publishes a booklet for the Catholic motorist prescribing rules for his behaviour and citing medieval authorities for his obedience to the Highway Code, the unsympathetic non-Catholic laughs at the absurdity. Is this the Catholic Church doing its bit to bring home to the conscience of the motorist his responsibility for safety on the roads? Is this an authoritarian and absolutist institution pretending to rule over a lost province? Is this the Holy Mother telling her children how to go on in the world? However regarded, it looks absurd. The Highway Code could not have had to be negotiated with the Catholic Church. The Highway Code does not need and can gain nothing from the blessing and the sanction of religion. It exists solely to reconcile and regulate the interests of all road users equally. Its efficacy in their interest depends wholly on their equal acceptance and observance of it. General utility is its *raison d'être* and its sanction. This public machinery for private living is kept in working order by the faithful observance of all parties, and serves equally journeys undertaken for moral and immoral purposes, arrivals welcome and unwelcome. But the Code itself is an important department of public morals.

The Highway Code is a model example of politico-technical rules as the basis of social cooperation. Rules of the road are technical because they are related to the conditions they govern – although of course they are partly conventional and could be different, and on the Continent they are different. They are political because they can be modified by political procedures. The Code makes a model example because of its completeness and immediacy: anyone can see at once that such a code is necessary, that it is equally in the interests of all, and that everyone who takes a vehicle on the highway is therefore morally as well as legally bound by it and should observe it faithfully and see that others do so as well. Because it is immediately self-justifying like a machine the irrelevant intrusion of religious justifications and sanctions is obviously absurd.

The Code is equally in the interests of all. This is not perfectly true. The expert driver in charge of a high-powered car is restricted on the motorway because less expert drivers are liable not to remain in charge of their high-powered cars. There are these inequities. There will be improved roadways and driving conditions and improved car designs. There may be improved standards of skill in driving. There will be gathering experience of what happens on the roads, when and where and how. All this means that the Code is a better model of social rules for not being once-for-all perfect, in being open to criticism and adaptable to new conditions in the light of experience. The revision of the Code is a political process that follows the agreed political procedures.

The Code can also be taken as a model example of how politico-technical rules are moral rules. They are moral rules because in the case of the Code they are agreed by all those whose interests are affected by them, all road users, and they can be modified by, and modified only by, agreed procedures; and therefore all road users are responsible for observing them in good faith and responsible for seeing that others observe them also, since the rationale and efficacy of the rules depend entirely on equal responsibility and mutual good faith. Correct behaviour on the roads as strict observance of the rules of the Code, in so far as it is general, tends to produce good-tempered, even joyful, driving, a *camaraderie*, a sociability of the road, a motoring community with standards of amenity and courtesy. Thus the politico-technical rules which have legal force, when they are morally upheld and observed by each in the interests of all tend to produce a community with sympathetic bonds and characteristic graces. Certain *values* emerge and become established, traditions of the road which reinforce and enhance the rules. The model illustrates the principles equally well negatively when one sees the rules flagrantly flouted and road-hogs and reckless drivers in number increasing the hazards and diminishing the pleasures of driving until there is little incentive to maintain decent standards and every driver regards every other with suspicion or hostility.

Politico-technical rules of social cooperation when they are morally upheld and faithfully observed, although they are very different in character and rationale from religious customs and beliefs which bind a whole society and its generations, are not less powerfully binding, for they are rooted in utility and common interest, they constitute society, and they evoke public spirit and create community. All this does not follow automatically; it only follows if the politico-technical rules are morally upheld and highly valued. This can only happen if the rules serve and are felt to serve the interests of those who are bound by them. In the case of the Highway Code this clearly does happen; and even in this simplest of cases the result so far is no better than mediocrity.

There are two main types of social rules: those which regulate what one wants to do so that one does not come into collision with others doing what they want to do; those which regulate cooperation for some common purpose. By analogy, the first may be called 'rules of the road' (avoiding collision), the second 'rules of the game' (common purpose). The first kind involve cooperation and interdependence, but the cooperation is facilitating solo operations and the interdependence is supporting independence. Rules for the conduct of business in a public meeting or a committee are of the first kind, in that different persons or factions want to make themselves heard and to get their own way, and the rules allow all to try to do this and regulate how it shall be done. Judicial rules to ensure fair trial are of the first kind, enabling an aggrieved party or the State to seek justice without injury to legitimate interests. Resolutions of a public meeting, decisions of a committee, are rules of the second kind, authorizing and governing actions for a common purpose. Similarly, the political rules of a free society are of the first kind, regulating the pushes and pulls of organized interests in their attempts to prevail and to get what they want; whereas enactments of parliament and settled public policies are rules of the second kind governing common social purposes and the appropriate common action. The common purposes are only provisional or conventional common purposes since they are open to attempts at revision or repeal by the political rules, but in so far as they are genuine compromises they may be effective and lasting common purposes. Rules of the first kind might be called 'liberal' rules, since the classical liberal ideal was to reduce all social rules to rules of this kind; and rules of the second type might be called 'socialist' rules, since the classical socialist ideal was to regulate all society by rules of this kind. Both the classical ideals are dreams. We need not say whether nightmares or visions of utopia.

Of course 'rules of the road' *may* be described as rules for cooperation serving a common purpose, and the rules of politics may look at first sight as the best example of 'rules of the game'. That is only to say that distinctions and analogies serve very well until they are pressed too far. In this case the distinction made by the analogies remains, and remains important. However, the distinction is not made in a closed society, where there are no 'rules of the road'. The Roman Catholic leaflet is an indication of that. And although the distinction is a characteristic of an open society, there is no final distinction because all rules ultimately are justified in an open society only by the purpose of enabling all individuals and groups to do what they want to do, so far as this is possible. 'Rules of the game' in an open society are not really rules of a game which is final, a common purpose sufficient for its own sake: they are rules for cooperation in a common purpose (say, old-age pensions or the defence of Malaysia) that serve particular interests or the general interest in a way that is agreed by the political rules. In an open society there is no 'game' for its own sake constituted by its rules. All the rules are ultimately for the sake of enabling people to get what they want and do what they want, whether one for himself or in association one with another. This ultimate permissiveness of the open society is of course 'ultimate' as it has to be if *all* people are to enjoy the same liberty, and because short-term interests are often in conflict with long-term interests and people have to learn what they really do want to get or to do.

In an open society the rules are morally binding only in so far as they are agreed by the political or other procedures for reaching agreement; and agreement is not likely to be reached unless the interests affected by the rules are adequately represented. Put crudely, the rule against stealing is not morally binding for anyone who has no property of his own and no legitimate means of acquiring any. He is outside the society in which the rule protects the interests of its members. An incomes policy may be requisite if a 'managed' economy is to be managed and inflation controlled, but the rules established by such a policy are not likely to be felt as morally binding unless they are agreed, and agreement does not mean a 'leonine' bargain. A highly populated, highly organized industrial society will depend increasingly for its order and efficiency upon such agreements freely negotiated. Interdependence expressed and constituted in agreed rules is the foundation of the open society.

Independence Based upon Interdependence

The Utilitarian social philosophy of Jeremy Bentham, leavened and made wholesome by John Stuart Mill's postscript 'On Liberty', translated into a modern idiom and brought up to date with new possibilities, new necessities and new dangers, is the humanist social philosophy today, and substantially will be permanently so. The criterion is 'utility' which Bentham humanized in the borrowed phrase 'the greatest happiness of the greatest number', and 'each is to count for one and no one for more than one'. Also, in this philosophy rules (laws) are a necessary evil, and the fewer the better.

'Happiness' of course is the trickiest of concepts. As a private not a public thing it is perhaps not the most useful political concept. Liberty is part of the public side of it, for one has to be free to pursue one's own happiness in one's own way; and one requires the means to be able to enjoy or do what one wants. A. N. Whitehead defined liberty in concrete terms as 'practicability of purpose', being able to do what one wants to do – being allowed to and having the means to. 'The greatest happiness of the greatest number' might be given more concreteness as 'more people able to do more things'. This multiplication of choices can be increased by society more directly and definitely than the promotion of the greatest happiness. More people able to own motor cars might be taken as a stultification of the principle straightway in an obvious and painful example. However, the stultification is not a stultification of the principle, a *reductio ad absurdum*, but stultification of a society that will not deal with its basic problems, in this case, a runaway population, 'traffic in towns', conurbations, congested highways. This single complex problem of population-cum-traffic can stand for the required long-term redesigning of the common life in terms of agreed physical conditions, as the Highway Code represents the required agreed rules for going our separate ways together. Designing our basic interdependence by instituting agreed rules and creating agreed physical conditions brings about a stable and productive society, stable because productive and productive in the broad sense of enabling more people to do more things.

Redesign by agreement is a far-reaching process of reordering a traditional society; far-reaching and long-term, for there is never a clean slate. Moreover, agreement does not lie between individuals and the State, in the direct way in which eighteenth-century democrats thought of it. Rather, society is a congeries of groups, as Burke thought of it (the 'small platoon'), families, churches, neighbourhoods, cities, trade unions, clubs and associations of all kinds. Most agreements are in effect the outcome of negotiations of groups with other groups on behalf of their members, even when the agreement has the form of a statute. All these groups within national frontiers will share a 'culture' or common way of life, expressed in language, religion, history, institutions, norms and expectations of behaviour. There will be class, local, and other variants of the national culture, but they will be seen as varieties of the same thing by contrast with the different

from them, there is no genuine mutuality of interests, no bargain; it is a constraint not a contract. Of course the force of constraint can be concealed from those it binds by appeals to deeper natural and moral bonds. At the same party congress, Mikhail Sholokhov denounced the gaoled writers Andrei Sinyavsky and Yuli Daniel as 'a-moral', as having 'slung mud at everything most sacred to us', as guilty of the most 'sacrilegious' act in raising a hand against their mother, the Soviet homeland. These religious and moral categories are wielded to overthrow the will and induce total submission. The submission of one requires the submission of all. For the system itself has to be put beyond question, with all 'sacred' things.

The open society is not a 'sacred' society. Its viability depends solely upon its acceptability. Founded in utility, it is a contract. As a necessary contract and a valued contract, it is sustained by and sustains good faith, and expresses itself in good manners and protects itself by public spirit. Unless it does have this healthy acceptability and this spontaneous grace, the open society is in danger of becoming insecure and having to repair to coercive measures – a state of affairs like that on the roads when the rules are being generally flouted.

A society surrounded by a symbolic iron curtain or an actual Berlin wall is in plainest contrast to an open society. More useful comparisons can be made with a 'liberal' society and with a 'pluriform' society, since neither of these is a closed society and both are incomplete forms of the open society.

The *laissez-faire* liberal society differs from the open society in two main respects: non-intervention is a criterion of good government; interdependence is based upon independence. The restriction of government to defence and the maintenance of law and order and the provision of cheap and impartial justice in the courts is in any case a dream of the past. A mass industrialized society has to be highly organized, a mixed 'managed' economy has to be managed, a flexible mobile society has to have built-in provisions for change, the scientific revolution has to be brought under control. The automatic controls of a market economy on the classical model are no longer adequate, if they ever were. There is an inescapable social responsibility for the economy, for science and technology, for education and the social services, for social security. Professional services and social services (which have been professionalized) have become too expensive and too necessary to be left to private decisions and resources. For this reason, interdependence cannot be based upon independence, private initiative and choices. These values of a liberal society, private initiatives and choices, can be enjoyed by all in lives of independence solely on the basis of organized interdependence. 'Private ends (open to entrepreneurs) as public means to lesser private ends' as the dominant social pattern has to give way to a direct and more equitable service.

The 'pluriform' society is also an open society in that the independence of citizens and of associations of citizens is tolerated and guaranteed. But it resembles more closely the international 'peaceful co-existence of different social systems' than a fully constituted open society. It is an integration of communities, rather than a full association of citizens. Within the pluriform society there is segregation, perhaps of religious communities, of races, of minorities, of classes or castes. Groups of this kind may enjoy their own languages, institutions, customs, education apart from other groups or the main community. The toleration and protection of such groups and their ways may seem to be more the mark and virtue of an open society than is the agreed organization of interdependence in support of independence. These forms of segregation are indeed forms of independence. Are church schools, racial minorities, or social classes the glory of an open society or blots and blemishes upon it?

The protection of them from all forms of persecution, discrimination, oppression, exploitation can come only by their own political action, and this begins to create the conditions of an open society. They are hereditary communities, not associations for a particular purpose. On the principles of an open society should they be integrated as groups or assimilated as persons? If the virtue and value of an open society is the endowment of the individual with the widest possible range of choice, segregation in hereditary communities is a handicap. On the other hand, other things being equal, social class or religious community or racial identity may be a rich inheritance, a habitat within which one can thrive and develop, and without which one lapses into an impoverished impersonal anonymity. The Jew or Catholic or worker or Negro who stays within his community that keeps its identity is safer and likely to be happier than anyone who sits looser to such ties. Safer, probably; happier perhaps, because happiness is not highly predictable. But the very notion of self-dependence and self-government is a word of emancipation from such hereditary communities. In the open society their walls will not be thrown down, but they will be breached from the inside. Class barriers, religious barriers, race barriers are not easily, nor often rightly, assaulted from without, but unless they crumble or are dismantled the pluriform society does not become the open society, and until that happens everyone finds his identity more by chance than by choice.

Ethos of the Open Society

The practical politics of humanism will be considered later, mainly in terms of strategy and tactics. Here the political philosophy of humanism is expressed in the notion of the open society. The open society is not a womb, warmly secure and motherly. It is not a family, with Mother in the background and Father dominant. It is not a barracks, orderly and all round, doses of duty and doles of leave. It is a grown-up bargaining affair; interdependence is not dependence. But it is not merely a market, a *laissez-faire* affair. Underneath interdependence is a corset of hard agreements, but what strikes the eye is the grace and style of public amenity and public spirit which follow from general satisfaction with the social arrangements. This can happen only if all interests are adequately represented and can reasonably hope to be taken care of by that means. Those interests that are too weak to organize themselves for forceful bargaining – like pensioners, the unemployed, the handicapped – are taken care of because the open society is simply the organization of public means to personal independence and fulfilment, and 'each is to count for one and no one for more than one'. The open society is therefore a welfare society. Interdependence, although utilitarian, is a partnership in well-being, as Burke said. And, in spite of Burke, liberty, equality and fraternity is the sovereign ideal of human association. How to achieve this trinity in unity is the perpetual social problem.

Burke was right. The ideal of human association cannot be seized by any kind of revolutionary action. It has to be approached by an historical route. In this country today (at least in a humanist's view) the open society is our best possibility. So far it has not been decisively chosen. There is still established privilege, class and religious privilege, official recognition of a crumbling order. Society is no longer uniform, it is pluriform, but not yet open. Segregation is a protective covering, more likely to be taken off when the sun shines than when the wind blows. Mere hostility towards segregation (church schools, for example) justifies the desire for it. The traveller feels the wind and draws his cloak tightly about him. Whereas when private values are deeply respected *within* public institutions because interdependence is organized by agreement for the sake of independence, the sun comes out and the traveller takes off his cloak. This shared confidence in common institutions for all general social purposes has to be created. Humanists alone cannot hope to bring in the open society, for that is a contradiction in terms. It waits on general acceptance of the principle of interdependence for the sake of independence as a corollary of political democracy. When this pattern is socially established as a way of life, the schools, through which society reproduces itself, will be preparations for and models of the open society.

4

THE HUMANIST HIMSELF

We are, to the extent that we know how to be wise, the artisans of our own life.

Fontenelle

To live badly is not to live badly, but to spend a long time dying.

Democritus

The Person as a Work of Art

A CLOSED society is like a machine: all the parts are inter-related to serve a common purpose. Or it is like a painting: to displace a line or vary a colour is to disturb the whole composition. In the Soviet Union the Party is bound to take a line on, say, 'formalist' music; nothing can be left undirected. By contrast, the open society produces only shapes, outlines, rough-hewn blocks, mere possibilities from which anyone may select what he pleases and shape and finish it for himself. The person is invited to make of his own life, and therewith of himself, a work of art.

The person as a work of art may not sound attractive. One thinks perhaps of an exquisite with handle-bar moustaches, gothic script and cryptographic signature. All arts attract charlatans. What knowledge and skill are required to master the art of living well? Socrates, bred a craftsman himself and watching other craftsmen at work in Athens, asked himself that question. The craftsman has acquired an inherited and transmissible skill which can be relied on to attain a standard of excellence. Is it possible to acquire and transmit virtue with the same certainty, and thereby ensure that everybody will be able to learn the most important of all arts? The Socratic inquiry led to the theory that human life has a built-in pattern of good, a purposive design; and therefore there was a standard model for all, by conformity to which the good life was lived and the highest good enjoyed. There are two grounds for criticism of this theory of life. The first is that the virtues and values required for living well are not acquired like the knowledge, techniques and skills of a craft. The second is that there is no absolute built-in pattern of good, no design for living, no universal model. The humanist rejects the theory mainly on the second ground. The humanist when he thinks of practising human living as an art is rather in the position of the contemporary artist who has abandoned the traditions, the standards and the models, and is out on his own having to take full responsibility for what he does without reference to justifying precedents. However, the analogy is only partial. The humanist, although he is free to reject the standard models of his culture, is not really as free as the painter to follow his fancy. Apart from the sheer obligations of the realm of interdependence, there are only limited possibilities in the realm of independence. Even the ways of living which have already been practised and have been studied by anthropologists are, most of them, not real options for the humanist in a modern society. His view of the world is largely determined for him by scientific information, although he is left speculative elbow-room. His way of life has to be selected and shaped from practicable alternatives, rather than invented and projected on a blank sheet. All the same, mere rejection of the standard models can make all the difference. There is room and need for invention. Human living becomes a different kind of project, personal and creative. Indeed, a work of art.

For the Christian, the realm of independence is a realm of obedience since he has chosen the rule of faith. For the humanist, there is no rule here; he is following, and shaping, his own will, being and becoming himself. Nevertheless, the humanist begins and ends by being human, and he shares with all others the human situation, so that there are some general descriptions and prescriptions that apply even to 'the humanist himself'.

The Seven Ages of Man

No one can begin to think of shaping his own ends much before adolescence, and by that time his possibilities have been settled for him pretty definitely by circumstances and by others. So formative are these early influences and so decisive one's birth-lot that anyone may well feel that he has rather refractory material in his hands when he comes to do the modelling himself. A vast deal waits to be done to bring equal opportunity to all and to raise the standard of child rearing. Meanwhile, however, most young people can be enabled to do a good deal with what they have and what is open to them when they come to take a hand with themselves, already in the third age of man.

For human life is not a block to be carved. Perhaps it is more like a fugue. At any rate, it takes place and takes shape in periods of time over a sequence of phases. So distinct and complete are these phases that Shakespeare used them to follow through the image 'All the world's a stage' and show that 'One man in his time plays many parts' in the successive Acts of his life, in each of which he is a stranger to his former self. The infant, the schoolboy, the lover, the soldier, the magistrate, the shrunken senior, is each a different character distinguished by his time of life. The passage in *As You Like It* is a satirical sketch, the life-cycle of man the poor fool who plays many silly parts before passing through second childishness into the 'mere oblivion' of the final age 'Sans teeth, sans eyes, sans taste, sans – everything'. That man can do better is the hope of any plan of life.

The humanist begins his choice of life by choosing to live. On his assumptions he has the option. If the terms seem to him too bad he can reject them. To accept them is to discharge all grudge and grievance and exchange demand for responsibility. He has then always to remind himself that he is not bound to accept the terms, and life owes him nothing.

Although each phase of life has its appropriate characteristics, its own joys and prizes, its own tasks and discipline, its own temper and tempo, they are closely bound each to each. Particularly, every phase is largely made or marred by what went before. Each is a preparation for the next as well as a complete life in itself. Both the identity of each phase in the sequence and their interpenetration have to be respected in any intelligent plan of life. Childhood and youth are too precious to be sacrificed to the present convenience of adults or the later requirements of adult life, but if they are lived solely for their own sake later life is miserably impoverished and bitter regret is in store. Youth may be misspent in many more ways than one, in drudging acquirement of elementary techniques that will never be used, as well as by the lack of any application. A balance between what is due to the present and what is due to the future is seldom easy and always of main importance. What properly belongs to each phase in both these respects is therefore the first study in any plan of life. In principle, one is both enjoying the exercise of one's powers and laying the foundations of future powers. Enjoyment of the experiences one wants, fulfilment instead of frustration, may depend on doing things at the appropriate time.

Old age in Shakespeare's sketch, the penultimate stage, is a sorry decline. And so it is likely to be if one allows oneself to be overtaken going on in the same way with shrinking reach and relaxing grip. Unless one has planned and prepared for a new way of life in retirement during full maturity, old age is likely to bring demoralization and collapse. But it can be made to be a golden age, the consummation of a full life, enjoyment of invested and postponed activities and interests, as well as looking back on one's own and looking forward for others. And if one slides into 'mere oblivion ... sans everything', that is to be judiciously anticipated by a euthanasia.

Techniques of Living

The providence of a managed life is not everything. Prudence is not the most attractive and popular virtue, and not the commonest. But it *is* a virtue, an essential virtue. Prudent self-management as the utilitarian basis of personal life is comparable to contracts, negotiated agreements, as the utilitarian basis of social life. Both make the soil in which more vital and graceful virtues and values root, thrive and live to bless the world. The vessel has to be filled before it overflows. One has to be friends with oneself before one is fit to be a friend. Nobody else is responsible for taking care of one's interests, satisfying one's needs and desires, fulfilling one's chosen possibilities, making a job of one's life. Doing the best for oneself can be the best one can do for others. This argument can be sophistical, but that does not dispose of it as basic common sense.

Prudent self-management depends on techniques. A plan of life is itself a technique, a method of integrating the phases in a whole and ensuring that each is taken for itself. The moments as they fly are not detached and snatched, they are the notes in a composition that flows, recalls, anticipates and is enjoyed less in its momentary nows than in its recognizable spans, and eventually in its irreplaceable identity. There are many other techniques which help and enable one to make a job of one's life. Nobody can do much carpentry without learning at least the elementary techniques of the craft. Perhaps few people recognize that there are skills and standards in everything they are doing every day, including of course walking and talking. In most that is done there is commonly an absurd neglect of elementary cause and effect, and therefore a great occurrence of avoidable failure or dull mediocrity at best. To say that most personal life is lived at the primitive level of custom and magic is probably no exaggeration. It is quite possible and quite common to put more and more religious dedication or moral resolution into life without getting better results because one is repeating and therefore stamping in the pattern of failure, doing over again more earnestly what has not turned out well and never can – perhaps until accumulating guilt and despair lead to eventual demoralization and breakdown.

When anyone gets on badly in anything, not least in personal relationships, there must be ascertainable reasons. The perennial advertisements of books and courses on 'How to succeed in . . .' count on the fact that there are ways of going about things to reach a reasonable standard of reliable performance, and on the fact that people in numbers go on blundering and floundering in what they aspire to do because of an elementary neglect of the necessary way of going about it. The first step in any such case is always for the person concerned to stop doing what he goes about to do. This is the hardest step, the nearly impossible step, because habit is nature and to act against nature is almost hopeless ('the evil which I would not, that I do'). A coach (cricket, golf, etc.) or a teacher or a counsellor is nearly indispensable if one really means to better one's performance. Only an outside eye can see plainly the sequence of what happens; only an outsider can intercept the train of behaviour. In the case of a game the coach arrests and breaks the stereotyped movement that is so natural, and makes his pupil acquire in its place most awkward and unnatural stances, postures and movements, as the necessary conditions of control and power, founding new possibilities of precision, reliability, flexibility and range. Obviously, the counsellor is not operating just like a coach or a violin teacher, but he is employing a technique himself and inducing the person he is trying to help to rely on techniques. This may be merely for the solution of a pressing problem or the taking of a required decision, but in principle this is technical assistance in thinking things through, in carrying responsibility, in taking charge and managing one's life to ever better purpose with growing confidence and skill.

In addition to these particular techniques for the planning and conduct of one's life, for dealing with problems, for taking decisions, for learning from experience, there are general techniques for living, particularly ancient ways of attaining wholeness or serenity. It is said that knowledge points forward and wisdom points backward, meaning that scientific understanding and know-how carry the world forward in progress, but whoever wants to enter into full possession of human being has to go back and sit at the feet of ancient masters of living who practised and taught esoteric techniques of liberation and self-realization. Some psychiatrists have shown great interest in Eastern techniques of meditation for the attainment of certain states of mind, with release from tensions and normal preoccupations. Particularly, they have been interested in techniques for inhibiting the cognitive intellect and detaching the mind from the habit of conceptual thinking. The interest of psychiatrists in these ancient techniques is understandable, since there are parallels with their own art and some clues for helping their patients and some insights into human make-up and behaviour. But what have techniques of this kind to offer the layman? Does humanism adopt or adapt any of them for the education in living which humanism essentially is?

In the first place, ancient techniques of this kind are not to be treated as simply empirical methods that have been found efficacious for certain practical purposes, such as gaining serenity. They are bound up with certain metaphysical beliefs: for example, that conceptual thinking blocks access to Being, or that the self needs to be withdrawn from its preoccupations and released for union with the not-self. These techniques presuppose some form of 'the Perennial Philosophy', the immemorial view that recognizes in the human being an element or identity cognate with the Ground of all being, and the way of life which seeks the union or reunion of the detached and disciplined self with this Ground, of human being with Being. The assumptions of the Perennial Philosophy in all its forms are contrary to the assumptions of humanism, and therefore it would seem that all these dependent disciplines and techniques of withdrawal and concentration are of no use nor interest to humanists. Just as prayer and worship can hardly have practical value apart from the theological beliefs which they express, and just as the Stoic way of life or the Epicurean way of life had no sense apart from Stoic or Epicurean philosophy, so, it would seem, techniques for living in the traditions of the East have no relevance to the modern West represented in humanism.

All the same, there is a permanent practical truth about human living which underlies these techniques and their philosophies. Access to the inner world of past experience and to the outer world of possible experience tends to be blocked or limited and needs to be deliberately opened. The phased plan of life which links the present with the past and the future is a fundamental technique which gives an orientation and a contemplative and practical grasp of one's life as a whole, so that one lives as the owner of more than is currently available. But this needs to be supplemented by certain other habits of mind which help to widen and maintain access to the inner and outer worlds.

Successive experiences push one another into oblivion, as it were, so that most of what happens soon becomes remote and is not readily recalled. What is important is that experience shall be available when it is relevant. This does usually happen in the solution of a problem. Once the problem has been disentangled so that it is clear precisely what the question is, what one is looking for, there follows a relaxation of attention which allows a kind of sifting of stored experience for anything relevant to the problem, which is likely to come up with some intuition or insight that provides a clue to be followed. The rudiments of a solution are discerned in so far as one's experience can provide them. A mind too fully made up, a life dominated by rules and settled ideas and rational plans, blocks off a great part of the inner realm of stored experience. Detachment, withdrawal, questions, are ways of making room for new insights, intuitions, starting-points, evacuations, which are acceptable because they are one's own, significant because they come out of one's experience and are relevant to one's concerns. This breaking off to listen to oneself, to question oneself, this switching off the beam of attention and the force of intention is a useful corrective and complement to purposive thinking and constant activity.

Similarly, one may remain blind to what is there outside because of set views and preoccupations or because of ignorance. An ignoramus may go round the world and come back little the wiser. Having nothing inside he takes nothing in. On the other hand, if you already know how things are you may fail to see how they are even when you are studying what is there. Early science is full of examples. A seeing eye has to be both 'informed' and 'innocent'. Again, it is the mind that questions and listens, withdraws from what it knows, is hospitable to new impressions, is willing to entertain and test unlikely ideas, that keeps in touch with the world and frequently wakens experience with surprise.

All this does not discount the value of purposive thinking and rational activity, as though the best part of the self lies submerged in the sub-conscious and the best part of the world lies outside the path of the beam of attention. This is one of the superstitions which discredit attempts to bring into play the whole of the self and to enlarge apprehension of the world. After all, one is only speaking here again of 'the open mind', a rational ideal. Purposive thinking and rational activity need this corrective and supplement, or they are cut off from their roots in experience and dry up. In keeping open to themselves and open to the world, that is, open to former experience and to new experience, humanists do not need certain set techniques like yoga, but rather a perpetual alertness, a willingness to break off and put at a distance one's most settled and cherished ideas and the world with which they put one in touch, a refusal to be fully identified with any idea or any experience of the world.

Balance

A human being, it has already been said, should try to maintain a temporal balance in his life, so that each phase of his development is lived and enjoyed for its own sake and at the same time draws on the past and prepares for the future. This is a main condition of identity, continuity and achievement. Another main form of balance is between independence and interdependence, personal interests and social responsibility. The rules for living and working together which express and regulate our interdependence are a necessary condition of independence in a modern society, and therefore the public spirit with which we observe them faithfully ourselves and require others to do the same is merely a recognition that all should be equally free to pursue their own interests. It is the spirit of good faith and fair-mindedness among equals, and it is whole-hearted and unreserved. Either it is there altogether or it is not there at all. Therefore there is no call here for a balance between independence and interdependence: the two are reciprocal. But apart from this public spirit that

keeps the rules and sees that others also do so there may b
voluntary social service in aid of those who need help, whic
draws on time and resources and does call for a balance, sinc
it is more or less, not all or none.

This personal dependence one on another as distinct fror
political interdependence is not measurable and cannot b
regulated by rules. Very, very many people suffer sever
handicaps of birth or misfortune, not to speak of their ow
failures and follies, which ask to be relieved if they are not t
be left to endure a lot of unspeakable hardness. Of course
Welfare State is an attempt to reduce this dependency t
measure and to rule: I pay my rates and taxes, and am quit c
this obligation. But the obligation cannot be altogether dis
posed of in this way, because the need is too extensive and to
personal and because it exists also and in greater measure fa
beyond the frontiers of the Welfare States. The individual i
left to say what he will do about it on his own. At the extremes
he is not prepared to do anything or he decides to live with an
for others a life of total service. Neither extreme is a characten
istic humanist choice. Total disregard of the immeasurabl
demands of human need is not characteristic because human
ism is an acceptance of responsibility for the life of mankin
and acknowledges a sense of human solidarity. Total service
which amounts to a total disregard of one's own interests, i
not characteristic because the pursuit of a chosen excellence, th
cultivation of enjoyment, the development of one's own re
sponse to the world, are ways in which one knows and affirn
the final value of human life. To devote oneself solely to th
supposed good of others is too likely to be an inauthentic life
an avoidance of the issue. Perhaps this is what is really mear
by 'living on Christian capital'. For it is quite otherwise fc
the Christian who in the grace of God already enjoys th
supreme and only good, and therefore can live wholly to see
the same good for others. The humanist must verify for him
self the final value of human life in his own experience an
purposes before he can have reasonable confidence that th
human lot is worth redeeming.

There can be no prescription of the 'right' balance betwee

which means not to be forfeited. The first law of nature (when people spoke of 'natural law') was said to be self-preservation, and the self to be preserved is not merely the body, nor life and property, but mainly the self that can always draw off and stand alone, and dare decide and choose for itself. This is easy enough in trivial things and may be not too hard in more or less heroic cases. A man forgoes his tobacco during Lent or, in Ghana, pours out on the ground a bottle of whisky in a jubilant libation for the fall of Nkrumah; or he stands against the entire community on the ground of conscience – for example, in South Africa he is against apartheid. For the rest, he goes along with others, he fulfils the usual expectations, he is 'other-directed'. His interests and pleasures and tastes and pursuits are imitated rather than chosen. He remains unexplored and undiscovered to himself. He is perpetually reiterated without being identified.

The artist, in a good case, is the typical figure of one who does follow his own bent and fulfils himself in experience and in achievement in a self-chosen way. This is not the waywardness nor privilege of genius, to be envied or forgiven, for it is the birthright or vocation of all. To follow that path, however, requires both discipline and moral courage, some ruthlessness with oneself as well as with others, for it is a realistic pursuit that is not justified if one indulges in illusions about one's possibilities. Against the devotion of resources to this solitary pursuit the interests of others have their claim, the immense human need that is far away and inaudible as well as the interests of those to whom one is personally bound: it is here that the balance is to be struck. If one denies oneself, not symbolically as in Lent nor marginally by pushing half-a-crown into the tin of a Salvation Army lassie on the appropriate day, but radically and in earnest, the well is poisoned: it is an ultimate wrong. To treat oneself as a means only to the ends of others, as to treat others as only means to one's own ends, is to destroy the source of value. That one can hardly sacrifice oneself successfully, anyhow, is no help, because that only means that one does assert oneself in spite of oneself in uncontrolled and usually pernicious ways. To be a wholehearted and acceptable giver, the balance must be maintained.

Of course there are different ways of striking the balance and of settling the balance to be struck. One may avoid taking on family responsibilities, another may concentrate his service to others in one or other phase of his life. The whole matter is for personal decision: but there is no honourable way of avoiding a decision. The days are gone when the only interests that counted were those of a dominant person or group, the 'master' in whatever guise. There has been a Universal Declaration of Human Rights. They are not strictly 'rights' and may not even be 'claims', but they are indefeasible dues if all human beings are to be recognized and accepted as human beings. This is not something accomplished by a UN Declaration, even if 'dues' do in due course become established rights.

The Other

The need for this particular balance and the decision it requires raise the question of the ground of the relations between one human being and another. Love is a proper prescription for Christians because God is love and wills love and those who enjoy God's love can will no other. The Christian has been told to love the unlovable and to forgive the unforgivable – and the humanist is inclined to add, to believe the unbelievable – or it is no virtue and no perfection (*Matthew* v, 43–8). Too many who are not Christians have tried to follow by going one better, accepting the command to love not only without human reason but also without divine reason. They seem to have lost their heads and forgotten what it means to lose one's heart. Love because of its long and honourable service in the Christian tradition is liable to be salvaged from the wreck of that tradition and, transmuted into a sociological concept, put to reign as the sovereign value of 'the sane society'.

Can a humanist accept the prescription to love his neighbour as himself? Here is a radical far-reaching moral rule which can be said to bear the universal imprint of the world religions is it warranted by human experience without the authority or sanction of religious belief?

To start with, there is the natural realm of spontaneous response and judgement. People like and dislike others, prefer and reject, warm and unfold in the company of some, shrink and curl up in the company of others, feel resentment and desire revenge, feel superior or inferior, and in general feel and behave in all the too familiar ways that characterize human relations. Some order and discipline in this primitive jungle is always necessary and is always found. The question is whether 'love one another' is a practicable and sensible prescription for reducing to order all these spontaneous responses and judgements.

Love or friendship as more or less exclusive choice of persons with whom one is identified is in its nature special, not general. And I cannot love my neighbour in the sense of giving as much care and attention to his interests as to my own and those of my dependents and closest friends. I simply cannot love my neighbour as myself literally. In this sense it is a stupid requirement.

However, there are certain important and abiding ways in which I am identified with my neighbour although he is not a chosen friend. However I may dislike him or feel contempt for him, however unworthy of man his behaviour may be, he remains worthy of respect as a human being and a unique end in himself. He is autonomous, his own man, a source. Whatever the facts of his life, he has human possibilities. However often he belies them, better possibilities are open to him, and it is in this sense that forgiveness is always due to him: whilst he lives the last word has not been said, and his future is not fully and finally judged by his past. These moral facts justify fellow-feeling and require a helping hand and imaginative treatment, and forbid censorious judgements, not to say humiliation that degrades or mocks his human dignity. I cannot love the unlovable nor admire what is not admirable, but I can indeed respect the human being in anyone and help him towards his better possibilities. Tolerance, tenderness, fellow-feeling of this kind is due from every man to every man, and the helping hand as occasion requires or offers. In any other sense love can no more be a universal due than admiration.

Humanist Virtues and Values

Although there is no definitive model for humanist living and personal life is regarded rather as a work of art designed in the light of a chosen ideal, there are perhaps characteristic humanist virtues and values, so that the lineaments could be sketched for a moral profile of the humanist. Let us try a deductive portrait drawn from cardinal humanist assumptions and attitudes.

'Open' is a key word. To the open mind and the open society might well be added the open heart and the open hand. The humanist is more than usually candid: 'This is what I think, this is the evidence I rely on, this is how I mean to apply it, show me where I am wrong.' He is ready to counsel and to be counselled, to accept himself as one among many, each to count as one and no one as more than one. He seeks equality and agreement as the basis of society and of good faith. He identifies himself with others in a common humanity sharing the same ultimate conditions. On that basis he is permissive and tolerant, loath to make an issue of disagreements. Because he is not afraid of pleasure he is not puritanical, but inclined to be gentle and tender and affectionate, to the point of indulgence. He would rather make love than make war – a vast understatement. Having explored and accepted the human and the personal limits of his life, he is active and effective within his scope, and cultivates appreciation and enjoyment of what he has, aspiring to be his own rather than to own and to share rather than to rule. Because he does not feel that life owes him anything, because he himself takes responsibility for it, he is giving and outgoing, and there is also a strain of endurance, long-suffering, in him. Seeing everywhere and always the causal relations of all things, he is understanding and compassionate; but he sees here also the clue to improvement and control, and the foundation of responsibility. He is thus poised between acceptance and aspiration, the real and the ideal. He does not worship and he does not hate.

Perhaps the virtues he characteristically admires and wants to cultivate are candour and generosity, fortitude and fairness, the 'open' virtues sustained by an underlying toughness. He regards truth as a primary value, but in the form of methodically attainable and testable knowledge; so that he does not think of Truth, Beauty and Goodness as absolute values, but rather of method, design and responsibility as indicative of cardinal activities. 'I would rather discover one cause,' said Democritus, 'than gain the kingdom of Persia.' The word 'virtue' has lost its virtue and become prim and prudish; indeed, it has for this reason practically passed out of serious usage. But the vital originality in a man for which it once stood remains the supreme humanist value.

Is this identikit delineation of the features of the humanist too flattering? Of course it is; just as St Paul's description of the fruits of the spirit idealized matters even in the close fellowship of the early churches to whom he wrote. A Burmese girl student of English literature at Rangoon University came to England expecting to find all Englishmen like Shelley or Keats. People with some or many of the characteristics we have delineated are likely to be humanists. Leave it at that without too much naivety.

There are a few studies.* Described in terms of occupation, class, age, sex and education, the member of a humanist organization turns out to be different from the majority of his fellows in being better educated, more often male, doing a more responsible or eligible job, and therefore in a higher social ranking. This says a little about the self-declared and registered humanist, but nothing about the humanist himself. An ill-educated woman doing menial work is not the typical humanist of this sample, but may be highly identifiable by the identikit delineation of the humanist.

The reason for making this point at the end of the chapter on

*E.g. 'Membership composition of the British Humanist Association' by Colin B. Campbell, *The Sociological Review*, vol. 13, No. 3, November 1965.

the humanist himself is to conclude it concretely by recalling the example of innumerable women members of the Ethical Societies of one or two generations past. Different as they have been in most of the ways in which people are different one from another, they have been alike in living their lives to the very end with a sustained inner discipline and serenity perhaps only matched by the ancient Epicureans. Without a trace of self-pity, and often with every excuse for it, they have carried on and maintained a daily face of cheerfulness and a constant exercise of public spirit until the last day. This impression has been so consistent and cumulative that it is unmistakable and unforgettable. Invariably, their secret has been that as young women they achieved independence of mind and decided for themselves the principles on which they would govern their lives, and thereafter simply adhered faithfully to them. No matter how lonely or hard the conditions of their personal lot in later life, no matter how grey and grim the world that closed in about them, no matter what they felt at heart, they had their standard, and conquered, not in ranks but alone, if necessary absolutely alone.

*

In this chapter it has not been possible to do more than post certain indications that humanism is a distinctive way of life. Although for each humanist this should be as personal as a work of art, there are certain traits in common which are formed by the assumptions, incentives, resources and ideals which humanists share. This way of life is original, distinctively different from, say, a Christian way of life, and it is as disciplined as a religous way of life and may penetrate as deeply into possible human experience. This has to be said the more sharply because humanists and Christians and others are going to have to work together more closely on the common human tasks and problems. They are beginning to pick up each other's clothes from the beach indiscriminately, so that they will be hard to identify on the streets. The Christian is already liable to think that he is a good humanist and something else besides, whereas the other humanist is only a good citizen without any 'spiritual' life. The situation is not really like that at all. Humanism is not merely a concern to improve the human lot. It is also a practical personal inquiry into ways of being human.

5

THE HUMANITIES AND THE ARTS

> Not the fruit of experience, but experience itself, is the end.
>
> *Walter Pater*

> . . . it is we alone who, swayed by the audacity of our minds and the tremors of our hearts, are the sole artisans of all the wonder and the romance of the world.
>
> *Joseph Conrad*

> Man's outstanding characteristic, his distinguishing mark, is not his metaphysical or physical nature – but his work.
>
> *Joubert*

The Humanists

UNTIL recent years 'humanist' was most often used to refer to the Renaissance scholars who revived Greek and Latin studies during the fourteenth to sixteenth centuries. 'Humanity' was distinguished from 'divinity' as secular from sacred learning. Humanism meant the Humanities, called (for example, by Erasmus) Good Letters, or sometimes Polite Letters. A modern humanist in this sense gives this description.

What is a humanist? . . . It is one of those terms, like mysticism, that are best left undefined. But it is easy to describe a humanist . . . A humanist is one who has a love of things human, one whose regard is centred on the world about him and the best that man has done; one who cares more for art and letters, particularly the art and letters of Greece and Rome, than for the dry light of reason or the mystic's flight into the unknown; one who distrusts allegory; one who adores critical editions . . .; one who has a passion for manuscripts . . .; one who has an eloquent tongue . . .; one who has a sharp tongue . . . *

There are in this description references to a particular technical craft, to the preoccupations of a certain period in the history of European culture, and to a certain distinctive

*Edward Kennard Rand: *Founders of the Middle Ages*, p. 102, Cambridge, Mass., 1929.

flavour of character, none of which has anything to do with humanism in the sense of this book. On the other hand, the description is broadly based on an interest in man (the 'proper study') as reflected in his own works of literature and of art; and these works of man are of supreme interest to the humanist in our sense. Why?

Literature and the arts provide the treasury and the cornucopia of human experience. We are humanized and educated in living primarily by our own experience but largely also by the experience of the race made available in these images of human life and calls and echoes of human thought. The sciences are one half of human resources, literature and the arts the other half. Human life is maimed and wretched unless sustained in flight by both wings. The Renaissance ideal of the 'complete' or universal man at least indicated this sovereign ideal which humanists are bound to acknowledge.

There is of course no possible conflict between the sciences and the humanities, but conflicts and controversies are always breaking out, and the degree of present estrangement between them has been the theme of Lord Snow's reflections in *The Two Cultures* – itself a storm-centre of controversy. Plato banished the poets from his Republic, and opposed training in philosophy to the training of the sophists (Isocrates) in speech and argument as the proper basis of education and public life. The Renaissance humanists generally opposed the dominant scholasticism. There are other examples. Looking back on such controversies one is almost bound to take sides because in the concrete case there were circumstances of the time which made the issue a real one. Erasmus was not against theology, but against pedantry, superstition and jargon with which contemporary theology seemed to him to be largely identified. Neither kind of discipline can ever supplant the other. They have common ground and they are complementary and mutually corrective – for example, the rescue from jargon and obscurity and the rescue from the vast and the vague. The 'plain style' was one effect of the establishment of the sciences, and the influence of technology on design was equally effective. Humanism is not and cannot be the party of the humanities nor the party of the sciences. That would be to blind an eye or amputate a limb, not the most practical way to simplify human existence.

Thus the Humanists are a dated phenomenon in the history of European culture like the Schoolmen, but unlike the latter their passionate interest in man and in the productions of mankind transcends their time and brings them into the partnership of universal humanism.

The City

The humanist as scholar of the Renaissance was a student of a lost and buried past. When Athens was 'the school of Hellas', oratory and philosophy were taught and practised as a preparation for public life, drama and lyric poetry were part of the religious festivals and games, Homer the primal classic was as current as the Bible in England in the seventeenth century, and all the monumental architecture and sculpture expressed and served the activities of the city. Never before nor since has there been such an integration and florescence of human activities and genius carried to the pitch of perfection. The Renaissance in Italy was also focused on the city and attempted to re-create in the splendour of the present the ancient ideal. In the great epochs of civilization the city has been the focus of aspiration and the concrete embodiment of the humanism of the age. As Lewis Mumford has put it: 'Mind *takes form* in the city; and in turn urban forms condition mind. . . . With language itself, it remains man's greatest work of art.' In the city, past, present and future coexist. The museums, libraries and ancient monuments in which the past may be preserved as dominant features of the present are in living hands to serve memories, interests and projects of active generations. The conservation and regeneration of the city in all its aspects and phases is perhaps the most searching test of the actual humanism of an age, for it is the web and the growing-point, and the truth-telling resultant of human endeavours and responses, and the lack of endeavours and responses.

If man is to be studied in all his works in which he becomes an object to himself, from primitive artefacts to the Sydney Opera House, the study is as infinite as the study of natural phenomena. These multiple studies can never be brought to a conclusion. There are no natural laws in view as the goal of such studies, no formulable truths about man. The humanities are not justified by natural fruits like the sciences. They do not have public utility. They are nevertheless 'the proper study of mankind'. For they humanize: they introduce men and women to man. Contemplation of man in his works, in the achievements of the past, is not to be left to specialists. This is an inheritance to be possessed, enjoyed and used. At the same time, if it is cut off from the contemporary works of man it is an escape into the past. The past works and the present works belong together and interpret and judge each other. The living city is the symbol of this integration of past and present, contemplation and action.

This notion of the city and of the arts as supreme expressions of humanism, and therefore prime sources of its inspiration, seems pretty romantic, almost sick, in the presence of the amorphous sprawl and congestion of a modern conurbation or even in the presence of what is most contemporary in the visual arts. This is humanism denied or mocked, anti-humanism along with anti-art: humanity with nothing better to celebrate than wedding or at least embracing its own fatality. The humanities is an old-fashioned name for the expression of comfortable relations of man with himself no longer possible. Contemporary art and the modern city blast the complacencies of humanism and question its very possibility as a serious answer to the enigma of human existence. Let us prepare for a closer look at this aspect of contemporary arts as a symptom of anti-humanism and a portent of doom, by a closer look first at humanism in the art of the past.

Characteristics of Humanist Art

All works of art in all ages and conditions of culture, as works of man in which man becomes an object to himself, are of human interest, and therefore of interest to the humanist.

Religious art is not rejected by the humanist along with and for the same reasons as religious doctrines. One does not refute a mass of Palestrina. All the same, there may be and there have been works of art which are humanist in spirit and character in the specific sense in which others are religious. Some examples of this contrast: Dante and Lucretius; Bach and Mozart; Angelico and Rembrandt; classic and gothic. Even to mention such apparently strong cases is to begin to have doubts and second thoughts. One competent art historian has argued that Rembrandt is in painting a counterpart of Spinoza, that he is reacting to the same age in the same way and expresses the same radical monism. The argument is fully worked out and documented, but it is a thesis; and books pile up on the other side, claiming Rembrandt as a religious painter not merely a painter of religious subjects. Geoffrey Scott in *The Architecture of Humanism* analyses the concept of humanism as expressed in the architecture of Greece and Rome revived by Brunelleschi and his successors. Nevertheless, this same architecture was used by the Greeks and Romans in their religious buildings and by the eighteenth century in theirs, as gothic in turn was also lavished upon domestic and public buildings as well as devoted to God. The nearer one comes to the modern period when a common faith is no longer unquestioned and society has become secularized, the harder it may be to find any relevance of distinctively religious or humanist beliefs to the work of art, save exceptionally.

Here it will be perhaps useful to compare the results of two lines of inquiry: 1. what characteristics would one expect a humanist art to have, judged by the general characteristics of humanism? 2. what characteristics are as a matter of fact displayed by those periods and works of art which have been given the name 'humanist'? By comparing these two lists of characteristics perhaps some meaning may be given to the use of the term 'humanism' in the arts, and some criteria indicated for humanist judgements in the arts.

Three main characteristics might be predicated of humanist art, more properly perhaps of the humanist artist, of which the first is strongest in principle. The humanist artist is not in his own mind and heart a servant of any absolute. He is not celebrating or decorating or expressing some absolute order or public belief, for example, the Christian myths or socialist realism. He is not an employee of any hierarchy or society. Of course the arts have flourished only under patronage, the artist is a craftsman who seeks and takes orders and in the great epochs has had hardly more chance of self-employment than an architect. But there is no room for the development of humanism in the arts until the artist can win a foothold of independence and follow his own insight, stand by his own critical intelligence, express his own responses, take responsibility for his own work.

Secondly, the humanist artist does not acknowledge absolute canons and conventions, is not bound by customary forms and subjects. At the same time, he is not a mere iconoclast nor a cultist; he is faithful to his art and he seeks a public; he selects from the past and he creates a future. He is open to stimulus and influences which enlarge his response and destroy pedantry and parochialism – what in taste is called catholicity, which is a kind of humanism. This set of characteristics which may be supposed to distinguish the humanist artist equally belong to the scientist. To be independent and responsible, empirical and temporal, relative and inclusive, open and responsive is to be a humanist in any domain of human activity.

Thirdly, the particular characteristic of humanism in the arts is adherence to the norm of human interests. The undraped human figure is the central theme and symbol of this interest, the norm in question; for the familiar forms which constitute the norm are natural forms rather than art forms. In literature and the arts there has been a descent from the grand, heroic, monumental and sublime to the domestic, ordinary and familiar, and this is a humanizing and a humanist movement.

To turn now from these supposed abstract characteristics of the humanist artist to the actual characteristics of works of art in the 'Age of Humanism' during the last decades of the fifteenth century and the early decades of the sixteenth, which may be taken as the period of transition from the medieval to the modern world, what have the writers and artists of this time in common?

In the first place, artists and writers at this time enjoyed a new scope and obtained and established their foothold of responsible independence. Civilization, rather than Christendom, became the dominant ideal. Culture in its own right had a status, role and power which rivalled Church and State. Therefore its adepts and luminaries were persons to be reckoned with, not mere servants to be put to work. Secretaries and diplomats were drawn from the humanist scholars and writers, which influenced both policy and philosophy. Popes and princes needed the prestige obtainable only by patronage which occasioned and rewarded monuments of genius. Poets and artists alone enjoyed and bestowed human immortality. The patron had forceful personal influence but was checked in his absolute control by the taste and authority of the connoisseur, and also by a growing public market. In these circumstances and helped by this interplay of influences, the humanists established their responsible artistic independence and found scope for their talents and interests.

Secondly, the arts at this time were not confined by any dominant clear-cut theory. There were four main models: the crafts (carried to the pitch of virtuosity); science (for example, Leonardo); rhetoric (Botticelli); magic (Ficino). This fluid situation allowed the artistic imagination to draw on all kinds of sources: nature, reason, virtue, beauty, antiquity, Christianity, astronomy, mathematics, machines, foreign objects and scenes. The contradictions inherent in this inclusiveness did not force issues at this time. Rather, it was the parallels and affinities which dominated. Music, the proportions of the human figure and architecture were variants of a single theme. Drawing was one of the main sources of knowledge and a key to general culture; its exacting requirements made a revolution in observation and scientific studies; art was science in action, directed to discovery and development. Conventions and canons had not been made rigid by explicit formulation in aesthetic theories. The one main traditional assumption, the superiority of the epic, had neither disavowal nor practical influence.

Thirdly, the subjects: nothing was excluded from representation. The patron saints of the Humanists were Orpheus, Prometheus and St Jerome, and no incongruity in the exemplars could disturb a common allegiance to rhetoric, technology and scholarship. The translation of St Jerome in the 'desert' to Jerome in his study repeats the incongruity, for both were staple themes, the one traditional, the Christian Father removed from the world in the wilderness, beating his breast, the other modern, the patron of the humanists working in his study as a contemporary. Of course St Jerome himself sustained the contradiction in his own person. The classical themes which in a similar way rivalled traditional scriptural themes were not only drawn from mythology but also characteristically celebrated the achievements of the Greeks, as in Raphael's 'Parnassus', the 'Disputa' and the 'School of Athens'. Or the same interest was directly presented in subjects taken from the contemporary humanist movement: at its simplest in Vincenzo Foppa's 'A Boy Reading Cicero'; with condensed iconography in Hans Holbein the Younger's 'The Ambassadors', in which the two diplomats are obviously humanists, surrounded by books, instruments of music and instruments of science. These were not dilettante career diplomats, but first and last humanists of the age, employed (often to their utter vexation) on affairs of state because of their expertise.

This engagement of the humanists in practice helped to balance with action the contemplation which was the supreme ideal of the middle ages. In the same way classical themes redress the balance with scriptural themes. The perfect equivalence is perfectly expressed in Titian's 'Sacred and Profane Love'. Here there is no competition, no sides are taken, there is no allegorical rout: the ideal and the real are presented with equal gravity. Symbolized in this picture, this treatment was general. Religious subjects were given a secular aspect because all subjects were treated in this way. This naturalism was the result of curiosity about and love for natural objects, and of the attempt to give to works of art the same authentic and full existence. Thus Michelangelo's nudes in the Sistine Chapel or in another dimension Hieronymus Bosch's 'The Temptations of St Anthony'. Thus the madrigal, developed from the Italian folk-song. Thus the innumerable portraits: the fifteenth and sixteenth centuries are 'full of faces'.

Humanist art is by no means all naturalism, however. The domed church on a central plan, for example, was a symbolic universe inserted between the macrocosm and the microcosm, but unsuitable for worship. And the imaginary cities erected at festivals or seen in paintings show that the ideal city was in their thoughts, perhaps as with language itself man's greatest work of art.

Virtue in those days was closer to its root in meaning, nearer to the modern 'virility'. The choice which merited praise or blame was between heroic energy aimed at achievement and ignoble ease, rather than between Good and Evil. Allegory was out of fashion. That heroic energy is brutally portrayed by Antonio Pollaiuolo, in 'Hercules and Antaeus', and orgiastically in 'The Battles of the Nudes'. It had titanic expression in Michelangelo's work and life.

The Age of Humanism takes its name from the concentration on man. The concept of man which was explored or celebrated or elaborated at this time was not specially Christian and was not specifically humanist in the sense of this book. The theme of the 'dignity of man' concerned his position in the cosmos; it was man in a cosmic landscape, and under this aspect it was his divinity rather than his humanity that was seen and stressed, although the inclusiveness and balance of Renaissance thought dwelt also on the misery of man, glorification was offset by denunciation. However, there was another aspect of man which was relatively new and which became a prominent Renaissance theme that is permanently humanist, namely, interest in the works of man, interest in *homo faber*. Connected with this was interest in man as having a role, a task. Again, Orpheus and Prometheus, the givers of discourse and tools, were the exemplars, rather than Jesus

Christ. Civilization, human culture, the city of man was the cooperative task received from the hands of the Greeks and Romans.

The Age of Humanism had a faith of its own which seemed irrelevant to the issues forced by the Reformation, and after the bloodshed of the sixteenth century it was the sciences that created the new culture and the new ethos. This was the background to English poetry in the seventeenth century, to John Donne (a relation of Sir Thomas More), George Herbert and Milton, all Christians *in excelsis* and humanists none the less. For humanism in the arts has been the exploration and exploitation of newly found human possibilities, whether it has included or even consciously excluded a newly found notion of man as a natural phenomenon not a divine creature. The arts in the seventeenth century showed the white-hot afterglow of the Age of Humanism, the baroque reconciliation of irreconcilables, glorious but intellectually indefensible, a representation of human dilemmas and tragedies and ironies.

By the time of the Impressionists there is a new public, the bourgeoisie, and academic canons and conventions. They had to break through and 'create the taste by which they were to be enjoyed', like Wordsworth, but although they were probably all humanists in their exclusive interest in natural forms they did not create a new Age of Humanism because by this time concentration on man was unnecessary and meaningless. The Impressionists were unselfconscious humanists, choosing their styles and their subjects, preoccupied only with technical problems, immersed in the simple, sensuous, passionate world of the artist. Jean Renoir's remembrances of his father reveal the exemplary humanist, living consistently without a theory or a programme in the plenitude of concrete human existence.

Contemporary Arts

Laissez-faire industrialism in nineteenth-century Britain was a destructive de-humanizing mania in the eyes of Ruskin that created a desert and called it wealth. The industrial blight and filth, the meanness and visual poverty of the industrial land-scape, the reduction of work from self-expression to wage-drudgery combined to make a picture of the degradation of a whole people. The artist in Ruskin and in those he inspired like William Morris (or Oscar Wilde) rebuked the present and borrowed from the past. Industrialism was brutal unless re-deemed by the love of life and of art; and art was immoral unless associated with the regeneration or the liberation of men. Both the exploiter and the exploited had to be saved from themselves by the artist, who alone knew what was good for man and what man was good for. Thus the artist claimed to be the representative man, appealing to and speaking on behalf of the artist in every man, who needed the social conditions in which to create and respond. This passionate affirmation of humanist values by nineteenth-century artists was in the context of a utopian socialism opposed to *laissez-faire*. Never-theless, *laissez-faire* with a multiplying population went on to destroy amenity and the human value of most work. How did the artists of later generations respond?

Partly, and importantly, with Non-art and Anti-art. This complex phenomenon of our time can be interpreted in many plausible ways. It can be seen as a frenetic nihilism, joining in the wholesale destruction of human values consummated in the First World War; or as a protest against this destruction; or as the evolution of painting from the Impressionists, pre-serving continuity with tradition. Or as the ultimate move-ment in the emancipation of the artist. Such generalizations are quite misleading, and to be strongly deprecated. Under-standing can come only from detailed study of the various movements and the work of particular artists. Let one of them speak for 'Dada', the key movement in the post-impressionist sequence.

Dada was the effective (and thus historically right) expression of a mighty surge of freedom in which all the values of human existence – 'the whole range of human manifestations of life' – were brought into play, and every object, every thought, turned on its head, mocked and misplaced, as an experiment, in order to see what there was behind it, beneath it, against it, mixed up in it: and in order to find out whether our well-known and familiar 'Here' was not perhaps complemented by an unknown and wonderful 'There' ('Da'), the discovery of which would transform our established 'Here-world', with its easily comprehensible three dimensions, into a multi-dimensional 'There-world'. Dada was a state of mind feverishly exalted by the freedom virus, a unique mixture of insatiable curiosity, playfulness and pure contradiction.*

Therefore Dada was not a 'style' nor properly a programme, but rather the policy of a few spirits who stimulated each other.

The essential was not the finished product: it was the creation of a state of affairs which made new products possible. Brancusi once said that it was not hard to make an object; the difficulty lay in putting oneself in the state of mind in which one could make it. The historical function of Dada was to produce this state of mind, and thus to bring a new self-awareness into modern art. Dada led to a new *image of the artist*.

The Dadaist . . . saw himself as an individual outside all bounds, whose native environment was unrestricted freedom. Committed only to the present, freed from all bonds of history and convention, he confronted reality face to face and formed it after his own image.

One thing he regarded with uncompromising seriousness: the autonomy of the self. Every spontaneous impulse, every message from within, was therefore greeted as an expression of pure reality. Every possible artistic technique suited his purpose of provoking these impulses. Absolute spontaneity, chance regarded as the intervention of mysterious and wonderful forces, pure automatism as a revelation of that store of hidden reality within the individual over which consciousness has no control – these were the techniques that opened the way to a more comprehensive view of the relationship between Self and world. The artist was free to turn either towards visible, logically explicable objects or ideas, or completely away from them; but he was free above all to come face to face with himself. Even though all the individual techniques used by Dada had had their origin elsewhere, and even though Dada's positive achievements

* Postscript by Werner Haftmann in *Dada* by Hans Richter. Thames & Hudson, 1965.

remain comparatively uncertain and elusive, it remains true that Dada's conception of the artist was something quite new. From that time onwards it acted as a ferment. Dada was the freedom-virus, rebellious, anarchic and highly contagious. Taking its origin from a fever in the mind, it kept that fever alive in new generations of artists. We set out to identify Dada's contribution to cultural history; this is it.

This is the apotheosis of the Romantic artist. How far it is compatible with the humanist conception of the artist is not a question at the moment, for it is given here as the rationale of current developments which describe themselves as Neo-Dada, Neo-Realism, Pop Art. These are at least partially disowned by Hans Richter, although he relates them to a mood of fatalism and life-rejection which he finds justified by the state of the world: it is a pathological art showing the symptoms of a pathological state of society.

Nothing is left to tell man what he *should* do; and soon, when he no longer knows what he would *like* to do, he will be in a state of total confusion.

In this state of confusion, the creative elements in the younger generation have made a violent attempt to recreate Something out of nothing – on whatever level.

The shock tactics of original Dada, making way for new works and new responses, producing 'art-for-a-day' (in due course for the museum not the art gallery), has lost its value with endless repetition and by being established. 'Neo-Dadaism is an attempt to establish such a shock as a value in itself.' This corrupts both artist and public. Nowadays we accept as normal the spiritual squalor of violence and noise, the lack of reticence and privacy, and the spectacle of abject infantilism hand in hand with great sophistication.

This degradation has to be taken seriously, but it is a grave mistake to see the contemporary visual arts as a pathological symptom. Dada claimed to be a new conception of the artist, and of the human individual himself as a completely inde-pendent autonomous being. This ultimate emancipation was nonsense, but the debunking of 'masterpiece-worship' which partly inspired it was not. The driving incentive of the Renaissance was the achievement of immortality through the permanence and fame of the work of art, the masterpiece. This idolatry had to be attacked. Insistence on the all-sufficiency of the present, creation of art-for-a-day, throwaways, mocked veneration for the work of art. Apotheosis of the artist in himself would take the place of apotheosis through the magic properties of his achievement. The new conception of the artist was an even greater folly than the old conception of the work of art. All the same, Dada did lead to 'a new image of the artist' which has enriched the old conception.

Of the four models for the arts recognized by the Renaissance – crafts, science, rhetoric, magic – the first three are permanent and are not subject to the fluctuations of theories and movements. The crafts and science, with the design inseparable from them, are built into our industrial civilization. Design is as fundamental as literacy or numeracy. Rhetoric, the model for discourse, communication, persuasion, expressiveness, is permanently necessary to social cooperation. Communication is the blood-stream of society. The fourth model, magic, represented the 'inspiration' that gives the work of art its power and mystique, and this was a more questionable popular model which needed the blast of blasphemy introduced by Dada – just as the 'sacred', 'tradition', 'authority' established in other places have had to be put in question and brought down. Destruction of the 'magic' model embodied in the cult of the masterpiece has been brought about by exploiting a less recognized but very old model for the arts, the festival. The artist as entertainer for the moment is thinking least of all of posterity. Vitality and spontaneity, invention and improvisation, versatility and flexibility, speed and dexterity, deception and mockery, exuberance and recklessness: these and the like are the virtues and values stimulated and encouraged by the boisterous spirits and ephemeral character of the occasion. The title Master of the Revels or Lord of Misrule sanctions the abandon, the topsy-turvy regime, the reign of folly. Moreover, there is room for all in a masque or carnival. Everybody competes with a contribution that follows his own line of taste or fantasy. The arts are democratized. This is the 'new image of the artist' exploited by Dada and its successors, an old playful amateur employment becomes established and professional, a recessive character becomes dominant. The play given in modern culture to the artist as Master of the Revels is an immense relaxation and refreshment, but if the artist is only Master of the Revels art becomes corrupt and corrupting. This is a tremendous auxiliary role (and like everything else in the modern world it is professionalized) which has brought lightness and quickness and frankness into our ways and dealings, but if the festival does eclipse the main models, as perhaps it threatens to do, it loses its sanity. In that case the arts could be seriously taken as a pathological symptom.

The Future of the City and the City of the Future

Although contemporary trends in the arts may not portend the fatality of humanism, an uncontrolled population and urban chaos may do so. The end that will come may not be dramatic like nuclear annihilation; it is more likely to be a slow erosion of all values, the insidious sapping of vitality by malnutrition, a mutual jostling and frustration, a lapse of all public spirit, an utter loss of peace, fulness, joy. If mankind is not to be overtaken by something like this ('not with a bang but a whimper'), it is recognized that resolute policies, long-term planning and specific designs are required.

The city of the Renaissance was designed as a work of art. One of its glories was to incorporate landscape design into the city. The park in the city and the city in the park are still features of civic design that humanize the urban environment. This was early linked with a humanizing of the landscape outside the city, and around the great house, influenced largely by painters like Claude and Poussin, Ruysdael and Hobbema. The other glory of the Renaissance city was the *place*, a precinct adapted to one or other of several urban purposes, public and domestic. These features of civic design, and the sharp boundary maintaining the integrity of the city withdrawn from the surrounding countryside, remain supreme urban values, but in most cases hopelessly lost and everywhere desperately hard to save. Correspondingly, the values of the countryside itself and of the wild places require conservation and are under constant attack and threat.

Modern town planning and civic design, inspired more by biology and sociology than by geometry, aim at public health and convenience and the accommodation of growth as well as beauty or amenity. The work of art has to be managed as a social organism. The city belongs to a region, and planning begins with a regional survey. The Plan incorporates past, present and future. The plan is shaped to the inheritance, to present habits and choices, and to trends and forecasts. The tragedy is that all the expertise, the team-work, the technological capacity, the prototypes which promise the exciting city of the future designed for living come at a time when their promise cannot prevail against the fatality of an explosion of population and industrial production. The problem is concentrated – perhaps it is better to say the battle is joined – in the single issue: traffic in towns.

The Buchanan Report together with the prefatory Crowther Report set out in 1963 with specific civic designs the feasibility of accommodating the estimated increase of population and motor vehicles over the best part of the next half century, at the same time improving accessibility and environment within the urban areas. The desperate alternative of an irretrievably ruined national environment by the end of the century was unhesitatingly posed against the extremely urgent, prodigious and sustained national effort required to avoid this future and to recreate the urban environment on the lines laid down. In any case, 'conditions as they are going to develop in this island in the next ten years or so will demand an almost heroic act of self-discipline from the public'.

At any rate it is idle to speak of humanism without bringing to the centre of its meaning today the concept of regional planning and civic design and the decisions and public co-operation they require. A design for living requires a basic design of the environment. The political and sociological concept of the open society, public order sustaining private choice, must include the civic design of the 'open' city defined by Professor Buchanan's concepts of 'accessibility', 'environmental standard', 'environmental management' and 'traffic management'. The cooperative humanist task bequeathed by classical civilization, to sustain a culture by which man is humanized in society, comes home with a shock when it is seen in these clear-cut terms of a specific achievement and a deadly menace.

6

THE HUMANIST TRADITION

Liberalis does not mean 'a believer in liberty'; it means 'like a free man'.

Gilbert Murray

The great conquerors, from Alexander to Caesar, and from Caesar to Napoleon, influenced profoundly the lives of subsequent generations. But the total effect of this influence shrinks to insignificance, if compared to the entire transformation of human habits and human mentality produced by the long line of men of thought from Thales to the present day, men individually powerless, but ultimately the rulers of the world.

A. N. Whitehead

Two Traditions

THE traditions of science and of political democracy, traced back to their sources and issuing in the concepts and practices of the 'open mind' and the 'open society', comprise an inheritance which humanists highly prize but which they share with others. Indeed, although humanists may be irritated by the claim that this inheritance is the progressive Christian civilization of the West, in contrast with the politico-scientific culture of Marxism–Leninism and also with the inert cultures associated with Eastern religions and even with Byzantine Christianity, and although any such claim would have to be qualified before it could be justified, nevertheless there is substance in the claim. For humanism in the West derives from Greek sources and follows Greek exemplars; it is pre-Christian but there was a marriage of Christianity with Greek culture, of Hebraism with Hellenism, which after the separation of the early middle ages was revived at the Renaissance and has survived, however loosely. This marriage was a marriage of affinities, a marriage of true minds in heaven, not merely an arrangement of convenience forced on the parties by the circumstances of the time. The thinking of Plato and Aristotle and of the Neo-Platonists and Stoics continually united with and fertilized the thinking of the Christian Fathers and of later theologians down to the end of the seventeenth century and after. When humanists think of freedom of inquiry and toleration, civil liberties and the rights of man, they think of the Church as obscurantist and oppressor and of the free-thinkers as bearers of enlightenment and campaigners for emancipation, and of course this is exactly true by definition if 'freethinkers' is used to denote these pioneers of enlightenment and emancipation; but was Locke, an exemplar of his age, truly a 'freethinker', or the founding fathers of the American Republic? These men and others who played an historical part in establishing freedom of inquiry and civil liberties were, most of them, religious men, though unorthodox, and did not repudiate the Christian tradition.

The peak periods of 'humanism', namely, the Greek Enlightenment, the Renaissance, the European Enlightenment and its prolongation into various movements of the nineteenth century, were in great part humanist in character, were certainly not specifically Christian, and were formative periods that transformed a dominant part of the original Europe of the Church into modern secular industrial democracies. This broad tradition, represented historically by 'The Age of Humanism' and 'The Age of Reason' and today by scientific culture in a political democracy, is broadly humanist and is definite and dominant enough to be clearly identifiable as the mainstream of Western tradition, although liable to interruption (for example, by Nazism) and exception (Spain). The 'open mind', the 'open society', and the sciences and 'humanities' are the glory of humanism and at the same time a widely shared inheritance.

Within this broad increasingly shared humanist tradition there is a strong current, an undercurrent, of humanism in the sense defined in the first chapter of this book. The Epicureans in the classical world and the Utilitarians in the modern world best represent this inner tradition and continuity, but there are other men and movements that share this identity. As a particular school of thought or 'sect' this tradition is narrower but more clear-cut.

There are, then, two humanist traditions, a mainstream tradition which becomes dominant in Europe after the Renaissance and a minority tradition which expressly excludes the divine and immortal from human interests. This explicit humanism is sometimes an undercurrent that forces the pace of the flow, sometimes an underset flowing in a contrary direction. The main patterns are clearly seen in Greek thinking before the advent of Christianity.

The Greek Enlightenment

The developments of the Greek genius which culminated in the Athens of Pericles in the fifth century B.C. have been called the Greek Enlightenment. Homer was the most formative influence upon Hellas, as the Bible has been on some Protestant communities. This epic celebration of achievements in the Heroic Age came to mean admiration of excellence in all human activities, in the athletic games, in the theatre, in building and sculpture, in oratory, in statesmanship, in thinking, in living. Devotion to excellence, cultivation of the highest standards in everything to which man's hand can be put is an educational ideal. Pericles called Athens 'the school of Hellas', and Hellas became the school of Rome and of Europe.

The famous speech put into the mouth of Pericles by Thucydides on the occasion of the public funeral for those who had fallen in the Peloponnesian War (Chapter vi) is not strictly documentary but it does document the humanist ideal of the Athenian Greeks of that age, which is delineated in deliberate contrast with the ideal and practice of their rival city-state, Sparta. Athens is an open society; Sparta is closed and rigid, organized exclusively for war, disciplined only in martial virtues and values. Pericles gives the picture of a relaxed society, at the same time ready and able promptly to defend itself and meet all emergency requirements. The Athenians are described as versatile individualists happily engaged in their private pursuits without comments from neighbours, their city wide open to foreigners not only in trade but also in the exchange of ideas. Eager and personal in their private lives, they were, as Athenian citizens, as ready to take their part in public discussion and public action, for 'we Athenians are able to judge at any rate if we cannot originate, and instead of looking on discussion as a stumbling-block in the way of action, we think it an indispensable preliminary to any wise action at all.'

This idealized model of the open mind and the open society in Periclean Athens is the main source of the broad humanist tradition. For both Matthew Arnold and John Stuart Mill, nineteenth-century apostles of humanism, it was the model that represented the ideal union of culture and democracy which they strove to establish in the modern world.

Thucydides' *History* itself is a unique humanist document, in its method and in its manner, mature and sophisticated yet fresh and graphic, charged with a sense of the glory and the fatality of human affairs yet accepting human responsibility and not overborne by the worse possibilities which too often took shape. For humanist aspirations the oration of Pericles is the script, but for the whole hardy and uncertain human enterprise the *History* itself is the documentary.

A very different body of writing has been compared with Thucydides in style and spirit, the Hippocratic collection which was probably a working library of the Hippocratic medical school. Some of these treatises are the most scientific of Greek productions, thoroughly empirical, in a tradition that has rid itself of irrelevant religious and philosophical ideas. They are humanist in a more inclusive sense than their empirical method alone would warrant, for they are informed by the sense of medicine as a difficult art that deals intimately and fatefully with human beings and therefore requires the most scrupulous ethical standards and the broadest human sympathies. The open sharing with the patient of the information available and of the intentions and thinking of the physician advocated in the Hippocratic school is an unsurpassable example of the candour and equal humanity which distinguish the humanist spirit.

Plato and Aristotle are the greatest names in Greek philosophy. Their own outstanding merit is perhaps a sufficient reason, but time and chance played their parts. The works of most other philosophers of a stature to rival theirs, notably Democritus, survive only in fragments, and in the case of Protagoras hardly at all. The thinking of Plato and Aristotle proved congenial to the eventually triumphant Christian theologians established by the Roman State. The tradition established by Democritus and Protagoras was anathema to the Christians. Plato and Aristotle are splendid luminaries in the firmament of culture, without question. Yet in most important respects from a humanist point of view Plato is the enemy and Democritus, of whom there is some evidence that Plato was desperately jealous, is the champion.

The pre-Socratic philosophers engaged in a sustained inquiry, striving by observation and reflection to arrive at an understanding of the cosmos and of man, disentangled from the traditional myths. There emerged an evolutionary view, with a main culmination in the atomic theory of Democritus, a naturalistic view which was purely speculative but remarkably anticipated the modern scientific picture in its main features.

Protagoras of Abdera, the city from which Democritus came, was well known in Athens, a friend of Pericles, and the father of the Sophists who went from city to city giving public instruction for a fee. He was said to have introduced the so-called Socratic method of discussion. From surviving reports and the few extant sentences of his writings, it seems certain that he was an agnostic and positivist and relativist, an acutely analytical intelligence with strong practical interests, the man who first proclaimed the *regnum hominis*. His practical interests were shared by Socrates and Plato, but Plato showed an intense dislike and disapproval of the teaching of the Sophists, which prejudiced later generations. Plato wanted to show that there is a divine order in the world answering to human reason, the divine and therefore immortal part of man; and that justice was built into that order and could be apprehended by reason as a universal truth, an object of discovery not an act of will, not a mere human institution or convention which could be put in question, and perhaps safely disregarded when nobody was about. He was looking for a built-in permanent foundation for society. When he thought he had found it, he had deserted Athens, the open society, for Sparta the authoritarian, tradition-bound, rigidly organized and disciplined society (in the *Republic*, still more in the *Laws*). Whereas Democritus had argued, and Protagoras in Plato's own dialogue of that name, that even the relative status of laws and human institutions is sufficient to make them binding because they are necessary as a matter of experience to society and therefore to the human condition. As Democritus had put it:

One must give the highest importance to affairs of the State, that it may be well run; one must not pursue quarrels contrary to right, nor acquire a power contrary to the common good. The well-run State is the greatest protection, and contains all in itself; when this is safe, all is safe; when this is destroyed, all is destroyed.

What is to be understood by 'well-run'? Obviously, 'efficient' but also something else:

Poverty under democracy is as much to be preferred to so-called prosperity under an autocracy as freedom to slavery.

And the function of law is not to make men good but to make private life possible for all:

The laws would not prevent each man from living according to his inclination, unless individuals harmed each other; for envy creates the beginning of strife.

Already in Democritus and Plato two permanent and radically opposed views of nature and man are worked out. Nature is a non-rational order which men can learn to use for their own purposes, adapting their interests to the way things are and adapting the way things are to serve their interests, all the time transforming their own nature by instruction based on experience. On the contrary, nature is a rational order, the product of a designing Mind, and man's reason can do nothing better – and in the long-run nothing other – than study and follow nature and fulfil the divine design. These two contrary philosophies in the name of Democritus or Protagoras and Plato fully represent early in the Western tradition the most typical and deepest division in human thought and practice, still unresolved. Plato's view leads to puritanism and all its works, to his own totalitarian utopias which look to Sparta rather than to Athens, and in Neo-Platonism to an alienation from the body and from the world. This is anti-humanism. Democritus, on the other hand, leads to 'the life of reason' as exemplified by Epicurus in the universal terms not defined nor confined by the possibilities of a particular city, and by later humanists in different circumstances.

All the same, Plato's genius as a supreme literary artist has enriched the mainstream of humanist tradition. His creation of the charismatic teacher and sage, Socrates, has been comparable to the Gospels. Nowhere else on the same scale and with comparable subtlety and sustained interest is there the play of mind and character engaged in serious if inconclusive inquiries, inconclusive because serious. The philosopher interested in the disembodied and invisible reality has given us the most real and embodied philosophizing, which begins with a sounding and examination of opinions with a view to going beyond them to certain knowledge, and most often leaves the issue of the discussion an open question. These Dialogues have continued down the centuries to exercise and excite young minds which would be revolted by almost any of the philosophical 'systems'.

Aristotle was formed by Plato's influence and retained to the end the same religious spirit and interest, but with a stricter intellectual conscience he elaborated his conceptual analysis and enlarged the scientific basis of his philosophy, using his metaphysical notions as a method and initiating new subjects for research. Plato's thinking led to theosophy and mysticism, Aristotle's to scientific research separated from philosophy at Alexandria.

Rome

Plato in the incompleted plan of the later Dialogues was using a cosmogony as the basis and proof of a spiritual philosophy. Aristotle shared this interest, but his programme carried him away from it in the direction of disinterested empirical science, and his system remained provisional and open. The later, post-Socratic, schools of philosophy tended to become self-sufficient and total systems, removed from further inquiry and research, providing a map of all knowledge and a compass for all conduct. Like the later Plato, they used a dogmatic 'science' for a dogmatic purpose. The most dominant of these schools during centuries of influence, Stoics and Epicureans, represent the typical contrary views of nature and of man which were found before and have continued since, 'idealist' and 'materialist' or 'religious' and 'naturalist' or 'humanist'.

The moral ideal of both Stoics (and the earlier Cynics) and Epicureans was self-sufficiency or independence, to be master of oneself and one's fate. In the view of the Stoics this was possible only by schooling the will, since over one's own actions and reactions one had absolute power, and over events none. However, since in their view events were ordained by divine reason (whatever is, is good), schooling of the will meant acceptance of what is and what befalls with serenity as a foretaste of the union of human reason with the divine wisdom. All men have in reason the divine spark and are equal and brothers. This is the 'perennial philosophy', the typical religious view of the world and way of life.

The Epicureans achieved their self-sufficiency on other grounds and in milder terms. A leading characteristic of Greek thinking was emphasis on the disparity between the divine and the human, immortality and mortality. This was expressed in such seemingly ethical but really superstitious characteristic Greek dicta as 'Know yourself' (that is, 'know you are a man not a god') and 'Nothing too much' ('don't get above yourself or the gods will strike you down'). Aristotle said that this was a superstitious view of man, for man really was god-like in virtue of his reason and it was his business to value and cultivate this divine element in him, not to go softly for fear of exciting the jealousy of the gods. Epicurus both emphasized the disparity between the divine and the human and disposed of the prevalent fear of the gods by teaching that the gods lived in a remote abode of the blessed and had no interest at all in human affairs, and that man was mortal; none survived the death of his body. These certainties cleared away basic anxieties and prepared the way for wise living. The essential needs of the body were comparatively few and easy to provide. Desires, on the other hand, might be insatiable, and would be insatiable if one allowed oneself to engage in the competitive strife of the world. Better to withdraw and live with chosen friends in a garden the simple life of enjoyment of enduring pleasures. In this way, by wise choice and avoidance, one could keep one's fate in one's own hands securely to the end, and die full and content. In the words of Epicurus: 'Friendship goes dancing round the world proclaiming to us all to awake to the praises of a happy life;' a simple, certain, practical gospel that was well received. Cicero said it 'had occupied the whole of Italy'. Epicurean epitaphs throughout Italy, Gaul and Roman Africa testify to its influence: 'I was not, I have been, I am not: I do not mind.'

The psychological value and validity of Epicurean teaching is easy to see. It removes the common sources of anxiety: fears of failure, guilt feelings, preoccupation with status, concern for one's role and the opinions of others. The dictum 'Live unknown' aims a blow at all the pretences and fantasies that build the house of cards in which people try to live. The immediacy of true friends and real pleasures takes their place and lasts as long as life. The simplicity, finality and completeness of the teaching made it easy to organize. Reduced to a small manual it was carried about and left about by merchants, and the groups of Epicureans meeting to read aloud and meditate upon the teaching and to share a meal together established the Epicurean fellowship, the friendship that went dancing round the word proclaiming the blessing of a happy life. There was more than a hint here for the later organization of the Christians. The great poem which Lucretius devoted to the Epicurean teaching not only carried it further by transmitting it to posterity with classical authority, but also infused it with a passion and pathos which it did not have but which it did inspire. The sane influence of Epicureanism is clear in Lucian and Horace and in Montaigne and Molière, and through these and others it has percolated down the main tradition – influencing, for example, Erasmus and More in the Christian sphere. Strict Epicureanism contracted out of the political world and was without public spirit and therefore 'deficient in the most material part of virtue', as Hume would have put it. To withdraw from the competition of the political world was to solve the most intractable of human problems by escape. At the same time, the disciples of Epicurus formed a community, a free and equal community which included women and slaves, and was unprecedented. Cicero, for whom public spirit was the pre-eminent virtue, detested Epicureanism as unpolitical, as well as dogmatic, superficial and uncultivated. Also Epicurus was the deliberate enemy of Plato whose school Cicero favoured. Cicero himself is the most representative and influential single figure in the broad humanist tradition. He 'received about the best and broadest education that has ever fallen to the lot of man', in the words of a modern student of the humanities. Versed as a layman in Greek philosophy and as a professional in Roman law and politics, with a strong public conscience and practical interest and a journalistic flair, he was well equipped to represent the ancient world and appeal to the modern. One of his works on ethics, written for the instruction of his son when a student in Athens, 'Tully's Offices', was extravagantly honoured in Western education down to the nineteenth century and generally regarded as the best practical guide to life produced by the ancient world.

Classical Sources of Progress

Christianity was in principle irreconcilable with Greek philosophy, as faith is with reason or the human with the divine. But a reconciliation was made through that branch of Greek philosophy which was a natural theology, whose Unknown God opened a way to acceptance of Revelation. But it was the adoption of Christianity by Rome for a military and political purpose that settled the issue. With the dominance of the Church, free inquiry was suppressed and survived only with the refugees from the Empire. In 529 Justinian closed the Academy of Athens. With the ascendancy of the Church and the decline of Rome, the elements of the humanist tradition – freedom of inquiry, political freedom and personal independence – were dissolved. Civilization as the human enterprise was interrupted.

In any case, it might be said, the ancient world had become intellectually bankrupt. Verbal philosophy had talked itself out. There was a circuit of five positions: dogmatic idealism, dogmatic materialism, scepticism, eclecticism, fideism. If one were young enough, one might be talked out of one position, or talk oneself out of it into another, but there was no exit from the circuit, except by a leap of faith. The modern development of the sciences, although they do not raise and cannot answer 'first and last questions', has made an appreciable difference to this situation.

If the classical world ended in intellectual bankruptcy and political breakdown (the 'decline and fall of Rome'), what was the achievement? Fifth-century Athens remained a model of the open mind and the open society. Looking back on that model with some veneration, a Cicero, a Plutarch, a Lucian continued to practise and to preach freedom of inquiry as a quest for a personal view of the world and a way of life, down to the time when the Church acquired the political power to discourage such inquiries and to prevent their encouragement. Greek science was groping and abortive, but one of the most eminent historians of science writes: 'Modern science is the continuation and fructification of Greek science and would not exist without it.'* Greek ethics admitted the claims of happiness as well as duty; and one tradition of Greek ethics found in the necessities of society a sufficient ground and sanction for laws and morals. Greek and Roman literature, philosophy, politics and arts produced models which posterity accepted and on which they formed their own ventures. These activities do not come to an end with their own success or failure. Their greatest success is to stimulate and prime

---

* George Sarton: *Ancient Science and Modern Civilization*. Harper Torchbook, 1959.

others. The word 'classic' records the pre-eminent success of the Greeks and Romans in their power to awaken and educate succeeding generations by their own excellent achievements.

Indeed, all the essentials of humanism in the specific sense were well understood in antiquity: the taking of all things as open to inquiry; the open city sustained by discussed and agreed cooperation sustaining independent personal lives, and as open to the exchange of ideas as of goods; in all things the pursuit of excellence informed by knowledge and techniques; separation of the divine and the human, with concentration upon the human – development of an alternative to religion; rejection of absolutes and recognition of relativism as a dependable and sufficient basis for knowledge, for society, for morals; recognition of a causal and material order as a natural and firm foundation for ideals and values; acceptance of necessary conditions and limits, and cultivation of appreciation and enjoyment of what is on hand and what is in hand. Piecemeal, they found all of it; and it is all to be found there.

Renaissance

The central and radial feature of the Renaissance is the work of the 'humanists'. The combination of circumstances that created the 'renaissance' in Italy already in the fourteenth century, like the combination of circumstances that created the 'industrial revolution' in England in the eighteenth century, has been extensively studied in recent years. The prototype of the humanists can be seen in the Greek sophists. The *studia humanitatis*, liberal studies, of which Cicero writes (the source of the name 'humanist') were developed out of the practical social need for letter writing and speech writing and making. The sophists taught rhetoric and the practical part of philosophy, moral philosophy, which provided practical themes of common interest for public discourse and debate. The intellectual result of this teaching has been recognized as the coming of humanism. Oratorical and dialectical skill acquired by diligent practice in linguistic composition was the basis of Cicero's own education and accomplishment. By the fifteenth century the term *studia humanitatis*, as employed in universities, schools and libraries, meant a corpus of five subjects: grammar, rhetoric, poetry, history and moral philosophy. The 'humanists' were teachers of these subjects, and also, as adepts in the composition of letters and speeches according to the established rules and the best models, were employed as secretaries and administrators and diplomats in the numerous Italian states. As students of poetry and oratory, and themselves composers of poems and speeches as linguistic exercise for the perfection of their accomplishment, they became not only connoisseurs of the classical models but also scholars in search of lost masterpieces and editors of restored texts. Thus as educators, publicists, scholars, ambassadors, official biographers and historiographers, civic and social spokesmen, they touched life and society at many points, and as basis and by-product of their valued techniques and services they recreated and cultivated broad fields of secular literature, learning and thought aside from and in some respects opposed to the scholastic disciplines of the medieval university. 'The Middle Ages surely knew Vergil and Ovid, Cicero and Aristotle; but we are indebted to Renaissance humanism for the fact that we also know Lucretius and Tacitus, Homer and Sophocles, Plato and Plotinus.'

The humanists introduced new attitudes, new standards, new methods. They established the professional methods and techniques and standards of exact scholarship, but not of natural science. They founded classical education for schools and universities. They made the extant literature of Greece and Rome accessible. They thus brought back into co-existence with the theology and technical philosophy of the schools a great body of secular general literature that was valued for its own merits as well as for its 'liberal' or humanizing educational influence. This was a cultural revolution which the humanists as professionals promoted, but beyond this they did not share a common outlook and they differed in their interests and activities outside the strict humanistic disciplines underlying this revolution. There was no basic humanist philosophy or body of thought. All the same, the humanists broadened the field of Renaissance philosophical discussion by bringing Platonism, Epicureanism and Stoicism into the question as well as the Aristotelianism which had been already strongly re-established. Renaissance Platonism and Renaissance Aristotelianism had important liberalizing effects. Another bridge to the modern world was a new speculative philosophy of nature of which the unfortunate Bruno is the best-known representative. The humanists in general were in the service of the Curia or the courts of 'tyrants', and tended to favour empire. Petrarch idealized Cicero as the 'sage' devoted to studies and contemplation, and was shocked when he discovered in the letters Cicero's passionate addiction to politics and the affairs of the world. Others saw in Cicero's civic virtue and patriotism and his republican repudiation of Caesarism another dimension of the classical ideal of human life. This appealed particularly to the humanists of Florence during the struggles of the city to maintain its independence. This 'civic humanism' inspired in Florence an emulation of Athens, a re-enactment of the complete humanist ideal, expressed in Leonardo Bruni's 'Oratio Funebris on Nanni degli Strozzi' (1428), a counterpart to Pericles' Funeral Oration written in terms of an actual parallel, not as a literary exercise in imitation. In this early chapter of the Renaissance there is a complete break with medieval political theology, leading to the autonomous politics of Machiavelli and the modern world, but meanwhile breathing new life into the civic ideal of classical humanism.

Later, the Platonism of the Florentine Academy associated with Marsilio Ficino and Pico della Mirandola gathered, focused and transmitted the whole tradition of Platonic thought. Both these thinkers were interested in syncretism and had a theory of natural religion, and in this sense were forerunners of the Deists and the eighteenth-century advocates of a universal religion.

Aristotelianism was not only associated with the study of logic and natural philosophy in Paris and elsewhere but also in Padua with the study of medicine. Pomponazzi was one of the most distinguished representatives of this tradition of

Paduan Averroism. He was more a product of scholasticism than of humanism, but he was touched by humanist influences and he read and respected the more characteristically humanist philosopher Ficino. Like Ficino and Pico he is concerned with the position of man in the universe as the principal theme of human thinking. Ficino, as a central issue in this theme, is at pains to show the necessary truth of the immortality of the soul, since contemplation of the divine is the end of human existence. Pomponazzi, on the other hand, developed an elaborate argument to show that on all rational grounds man must be believed to be mortal. The mind no less than the body, and in the same way, is adapted to and dependent upon the physical world. In further contrast with Ficino, he gives priority in man not to the intellect and contemplation but to the will and moral cooperation in human tasks. Pomponazzi admits that the immortality which reason must deny, faith may accept as a Revealed truth. Whatever his own personal belief may have been, Pomponazzi stood for the separation of reason and faith, philosophy and theology, the divine and the human, and prepared the way for a later naturalism and humanism more directly than any of the thinkers more influenced by the basic humanism of the Renaissance.

The virtue of the Renaissance speculative philosophers of nature was that they sought to shake off the shackles of Greek philosophy and to find new points of departure. Francis Bacon called Telesio 'the first of the moderns', probably thinking of his empiricism and his independence of Aristotle. At any rate, the Renaissance which was primarily a recovery and reworking of classical models of thought and art began in the last phase to find its own themes and starting-points and to be oriented on progress. The celebrated, but rather shadowy, 'quarrel of the Ancients and Moderns' was begun.

Francis Bacon (1561–1626), in so many ways a typical Renaissance figure, is the best representative 'first of the moderns'. And Montaigne (1533–92), a generation older, writes the best epitaph on the classical verbal philosophy and the reigning theology, 'que sçais-je?'. The two stand back to back, the one surveying and ruminating over the great achievements of the past, the other analysing the cause of failure in the progress of knowledge and proclaiming the coming and growing success by the new method of empirical investigation, hypothesis, and experimental test. Knowledge organized, tested and advanced in this way with a view to practical use would transform human existence and prospects. Bacon, although completely out of touch with current scientific discoveries and inventions, was the most articulate and conscious spokesman of the 'new humanism' of the Enlightenment that was in prospect. His *Novum Organum* (1620) is a manifesto of the new age, and a hundred and thirty years later in the Introduction to the great *Encylopédie* of Diderot and D'Alembert, Bacon is acknowledged and saluted as the pioneer of modern enlightenment. There had been no progress in the sciences for lack of proper method, because of religious opposition and obscurantism, and because of failure of confidence:

And therefore it is fit that I publish and set forth those conjectures of mine which make hope in this matter reasonable; just as Columbus did, before that wonderful voyage of his across the Atlantic, when he gave the reasons for his conviction that new lands and continents might be discovered besides those which were known before; which reasons, though, rejected at first, were afterwards made good by experience, and were the causes and beginnings of great events.*

The Reformation supervened on the Renaissance, and by forcing religious and political issues blotted out the humanistic Christendom mirrored in the letters of Erasmus – of which in some respects the Anglican Church remained a monument. A new world took shape in Europe to match the discoveries across the Atlantic.

The European Enlightenment

Bacon's reasons, like those of Columbus, 'were afterwards made good by experience'. There was a spectacular development of human knowledge in the physical sciences in the

Novum Organum, Bk. I, xcii.

seventeenth century. The period of 175 years between publication of *Novum Organum* and of Condorcet's *The Progress of the Human Mind* in 1795 can be thought of as the new humanism of the Enlightenment. As in the humanism of the Renaissance, certain studies were central and pervasive throughout the period. These were the physical and experimental sciences. Newton was the venerated name. His achievement was the model for all aspiring intellects. Corresponding to the 'humanists' of the Renaissance, students and masters of certain disciplines, were the 'virtuosi' of the seventeenth century, by which name were understood 'those who understand and cultivate experimental philosophy' (Boyle). Glanvill speaks of the 'virtuosi and enquiring spirits of Europe'. These were the founders and members of the Royal Society and of the Académie des Sciences. As with the humanists of the Renaissance, the virtuosi of the seventeenth century were not all of one mind in their general outlook, but were most of them religious men. Indeed, a main inspiration of the scientific movement of the seventeenth century was religious. God was the guarantor and the goal of empirical science. Science would answer the questions verbal philosophy had failed to answer definitively. Study of the 'word of God' had occasioned bitter differences, persecution, battle-fields, the dreadful conflicts of the sixteenth century. It was a relief to turn to the 'works of God', another road to God, an alternative revelation of God, just as valid, more cooperative and more progressive. The virtuosi were expressing their supreme confidence in reason (the confidence Bacon had tried to inspire) and in the rationality of the Supreme Being and of the work of the divine Architect. Locke asserted: 'No evidence that any revelation comes from God can be so certain as the principles of reason.' It was assumed that science would support Christianity, but it was the world-view of natural science that prevailed and the virtuosi tended to conclude that the propositions of natural religion (established by reason) were more important than the doctrines revealed in the Bible. As a leading authority sums it up: 'In abandoning the true ground of Christianity and arguing religion as though it were natural philosophy, the virtuosi did more to challenge traditional Christianity than all the "atheists" with whom they did battle.' *

In this way the virtuosi introduced new attitudes, new standards, new methods, as the humanists had done before them, and their work created the intellectual climate of the eighteenth century, the Age of Reason. The word 'philosophy' had a broader meaning in that age when physical science was called 'natural philosophy', and those who shared and practised the scientific spirit of inquiry were 'philosophers'. They were not 'rationalists' in the sense in which the great thinkers of the seventeenth century, Descartes, Leibniz, Spinoza, had thought out systems of truth from first principles. They were equally dedicated to 'reason', but reason was no longer a systematization of ideas given inborn in the head; it was active research, testing and doubting and finding out combined with the formulation of ideas, thus discovering or uncovering piecemeal the system of nature, including man. Everything was open to this inquiry, not least Christianity and every received opinion and established institution.

The French *philosophes*, imbued with this critical spirit (*l'esprit philosophique*), were the characteristic representatives of the age, and the Encyclopédie (1751–65) was 'the true centre of a history of ideas in the 18th century'. Diderot assembled a team of writers and artists 'bound together by the general interest of mankind and by a sentiment of mutual goodwill' in a venture that could be launched only in a '*siècle philosophe*', since it required exceptional boldness and independence of mind. All human knowledge, the arts and sciences, was brought within the scope of the enterprise, and what gave unity to it was man himself at the centre. Once again, the *philosophes* were sophists, diffusing the knowledge of the age, but even more eager to modernize the spirit of their generation, encouraging independent thinking, rousing enthusiasm for the progress of human knowledge, with a sense of the revolution that was taking place when 'philosophy' was being advanced by leaps and bounds and had set the prevail-

* Richard S. Westfall: *Science and Religion in 17th Century England*, Yale, 1958, p. 141.

ing mood, shaking off the yoke of authority and example and submitting to the laws of reason.

'Enthusiasm' was highly suspected and deprecated in the Age of Reason because it was associated with religious fanaticism of which the follies and iniquities had burned into the conscience of Europe. But in fact the age was remarkable for its enthusiasms, intellectual and social. To the enthusiasm for physical science kindled by Newton's dazzling success was linked an enthusiasm for man's political and social emancipation and moral improvement. Oppressions, cruelties, wars which defaced civilization could and would be abolished. It required centuries to get to know a fraction of the laws of nature, said Voltaire, but one day was enough for a philosopher to get to know the duties of man. The philosopher, he went on, was by no means an 'enthusiast', because he did not aspire to be a god nor to be inspired by a god. This theme, a Greek theme, an Epicurean theme re-stated by Montaigne already depressed by religious fanaticism, expressed the humanist temper of the Enlightenment, 'loyalty to one's own being' as Montaigne put it; 'the proper study of mankind is man' in the words of Alexander Pope, who returns to the idea many times. There had been a revival of Epicureanism in Europe from the middle of the seventeenth century, both for its atomic theory and still more for its moral theory. Epicurus, it seemed, had given a saner account of human nature than either Plato or the Stoics. The Christian estimate was reversed. Without pleasure and the 'passions' there were no springs of action. The human being was irreparably damaged by the brutal treatment of the Stoics (see La Fontaine's Fable 'The Scythian Philosopher').* But the new Epicureanism had a wider context than the Garden of Epicurus. The eighteenth

---

*When Hume was Keeper of the Advocates' Library in Edinburgh he bought a copy of the *Fables* of La Fontaine, which the Curators ordered to be removed from the shelves. In a letter to the Lord Advocate, Hume wrote: 'But this I will venture to justify before any literary society in Europe, that if every book not superior in merit to La Fontaine be expelled the Library, I shall engage to carry away all the remains in my pocket.'

century took a genial and social view of man. He was required to be an agreeable and a useful member of society. Lord Annan, speaking of Hume, has curtly dismissed this as a 'clubman's morals', in these words really putting it back into the Garden of Epicurus. But this judgement is unfair and unhistorical. The club standards were new standards and good standards, even sufficient. The dark underside of human behaviour outside the club was not unknown to Hume the historian; it was one of his worries. And Voltaire's personal life was haunted by it.

Victor Hugo said of Voltaire: 'He was more than a man; he was an age.' He compared him with Jesus Christ, and said he represented Man. Rhetoric perhaps, but a sober modern historian ends his biography:

How many saints in the Church's calendar have a record of service to man that will compare with his? His friends knew him. Here is the verdict of the ablest intellect and the finest character among them. 'If virtue', wrote Condorcet, 'consists in doing good and in loving mankind with passion, what man has had more virtue?'*

These words can be said seriously and truly of Voltaire because of his sustained personal campaign against the inhuman barbarities of the Theocracy in France, in the Calas case and those that followed. With the other *philosophes*, but pre-eminently, he moulded the liberal mind of the rising bourgeoisie. His model was England after the revolution of 1689, and the philosopher of the Revolution John Locke. Religious toleration and constitutional government, however imperfect, were there demonstrated as practicable. With Hume, the *philosophes* hoped, not to change human nature, but to change human situations and institutions, and thus to modify and improve human behaviour. By political emancipation and by education every man could be given a footing of independence and released from forms of dependence which kept him an ignorant slave, a tool, degraded himself and degrading his master – clerical or lay. Enthusiasm for this pro-

* H. N. Brailsford: *Voltaire*, Home University Library.

gramme of enlightenment and emancipation made the Enlightenment a golden age of humanism.

Bacon's *Novum Organum* was the prelude; the finale was Condorcet's *Sketch for a Historical Picture of the Progress of the Human Mind*, a poignant memorial of the *philosophes* because composed by one of the most brilliant and attractive of them whilst in hiding from the Terror during the Revolution on the eve of his death and because it is the quintessence of their spirit and the epitome of their outlook, and contains also a description of their life-work and their methods, 'taking for their battle cry – *reason, tolerance, humanity*'. Condorcet's purpose like Bacon's was to breathe confidence into men by showing them what improvement of the human lot was possible and by what means. His optimism is sombre and realistic but fervent. He combines a trumpet call with strategical and tactical thinking.

The Modern Theme

By the end of the eighteenth century the seamless robe of rationalism was tattered and torn. The earlier idea or assumption, that reason in man was a universal faculty in principle the same as reason in God and in Nature, was no longer tenable. Reason had become located in society as a cultural tool, rather than in the head of every man as an equipment of innate ideas. And the cooperative exploration of nature by means of the cultural tool was beginning to reveal an order that was not a rational system like a machine serving some purpose, but a biological and historical development that showed laws of a different kind. Darwin gave classical and systematic expression to the new ideas about nature as Locke earlier had given expression to the new ideas about rational knowledge. In Kant science ceased to be philosophy and philosophy began to be a philosophy of science, reflection upon our knowledge, rather than a superior kind of knowledge about the world. The critique of reason from within made way for spontaneity, individualism, the 'passions'. Romanticism was not merely a rebellion from without. The integration of reason and nature, spontaneity and institutions, 'culture' and 'life' became 'the modern theme' in the words of Ortega y Gasset. It is an essential humanist theme. For humanism is not to be identified with rationalism.

The direct heirs of the *philosophes* were Saint-Simon and Auguste Comte in France and their followers, and the Benthamites or Utilitarians in England. These differed from the *philosophes* in their thinking and in their method. Their aspiration was to form a school of thought that would furnish the intellectual and moral resources for a strong and convinced party in the country. The complete theory in the study, the party in the country, the party organ or 'review', the programme, perhaps a club: this was the pattern in the nineteenth century. The *philosophes* although not organized were a band of brothers and their propagandist activities had a common inspiration and a common aim. The nineteenth century 'schools' were dogmatic, exclusively organized and linked with a specific social or political programme. Many of them were socialist in character. The most thorough and perfectly developed of these schools was Marxism, with the working-class organizations it inspired.

The *philosophes* and the English Utilitarians appealed to and informed the middle class. Throughout the nineteenth century the Cooperative Movement and the Socialist movement in its various forms conducted an enormous propaganda and organized schools and adult education on exclusively proletarian lines. Over fifty newspapers disseminating Socialist ideas were listed for the years 1820–40. Most of this was secular and atheist, as the names Robert Owen, William Thompson and Thomas Hodgskin testify, and later George Holyoake. Charles Bradlaugh who founded the National Secular Society in 1866 was a vigorous anti-socialist, but an ardent Radical politician.

Apart from these schools of thought linked with their parties and programmes and organs of opinion, there were in the nineteenth century certain outstanding social critics who might be given the name 'apostles of culture'. John Stuart Mill, in spite of his close connexion with the Philosophical

Radicals, was one of these. Others were Carlyle and Ruskin, Herbert Spencer and T. H. Huxley, and Matthew Arnold. These men, too, were heirs to the *philosophes*, addressing themselves to the nation in the reviews and magazines and in their books, predominantly again to the middle class though in a different social milieu. They were not collaborators in the same way as the *philosophes* were. They attacked each other. But they shared the same ultimate concern and underlying purpose. They were resisting the destructive tendencies of the industrial revolution and *laissez-faire* economics – moral, social, physical and cultural. And they were anxious that the expansion and diffusion of the arts and sciences and of industry and commerce should bring joy and happiness and fulfilment to the masses. The physical, social and moral conditions on which the new forces of progress could elevate the dignity and enhance the worth of human living, progress and civilization as the humanization of man in society, this was their common theme.

Carlyle became eccentric and reactionary, but his earlier work was strong and valid social criticism. *Past and Present* (1843) was assimilated by Ruskin who acknowledged Carlyle as his master till the end. And Ruskin himself was the master of William Morris, of Gandhi, of Attlee and of all the many others in whom he planted a social conscience and a humane vision. *Unto This Last* (1862), with the message 'There is no wealth but life', preaching justice and humanity as the substance of morals and the quality of life as the substance of economics, and flashing a rapier round the pundits of the day, in spite of some nonsense and in spite of its biblical language, is one of the four classics of humanism in nineteenth-century England, and one of the most influential. Herbert Spencer as the arch-apologist of *laissez-faire* was not a humanist in the same comprehensive sense as the four others, but he did a great deal to modernize the thinking of his contemporaries throughout Europe and to gain complete acceptance for the idea of Evolution. Huxley did for Darwin what James Mill did for Bentham. He interpreted and publicized Darwin's work in a way that gave it ascendancy. In his Romanes Lecture

Evolution and Ethics he took the humanist stand against the ruthless 'social darwinism' of some evolutionists, including Spencer. In addition to his own original contributions to knowledge and his polemical writings in the reviews and magazines, Huxley was an educational statesman who did more than any other for the advancement of science by the reform and development of scientific education.

The other two nineteenth-century humanist classics referred to are Matthew Arnold's *Culture and Anarchy* (1869) and John Stuart Mill's *On Liberty* (1859). Arnold like Ruskin thought he was opposed to Mill, but they shared the same humanist fundamentals. Unlike the Renaissance humanists and the seventeenth century virtuosi, and even the *philosophes*, the nineteenth century 'apostles of culture' were not united and specified by the same disciplines: Mill came from philosophy and economics, Arnold from poetry and criticism, Ruskin from the fine arts, Huxley from the natural sciences. This growing specialization of the age accented differences but also called attention by a notable convergence to the shared fundamentals. They all transcended, and wished to transcend, party, class and school, and thought of themselves as engaged in a 'movement' preparing for social and political equality by carrying forward into the new democracy and making prevail the standards and the passion for excellence which characterized the great cultural inheritance from the Greeks. Particularly for Arnold and Mill, Periclean Athens symbolized the ideal of culture conjoined with the ideal of democracy, and provided a model. G. M. Young has said 'It is hardly an accident that ... the most conspicuous memorial of the Utilitarians is a *History of Greece*' (in twelve volumes by George Grote, 1846–56). Of nearer forerunners, the young Mill had remarked of the *philosophes* when he was trying to organize the Utilitarian Society in 1823 that they were 'the example we sought to imitate, and we hoped to accomplish no less results'. The decisive difference between the *philosophes* as a 'school' and the nineteenth-century schools, like the Positivists and Saint-Simonians and some of the Socialists, was that the *philosophes*, rather than a school of thought, was a school of thinkers who produced ideas by discussion and mutual criticism. By contrast the nineteenth-century schools introduced new secular dogmatic sects and absolutist cults. Mill was ever eager to keep the Utilitarians and Philosophical Radicals from lapsing into a sect, for this was incompatible with the ideal of an harmonious development of human nature in all classes of society, the ideal of Arnold and Mill.

Another shared symbol of nineteenth-century humanism, along with Periclean Athens, was 'poetry'. For Arnold and Mill, poetry (with which their own inner lives were identified) would eventually and desirably take the place of religion. Being and feeling, as distinct from doing and from thinking, was one pole of human nature. Imagination had its rights. The realm of possibilities was one kingdom of the real world. The union of 'poetry' with 'science' symbolized the completeness of a humane culture, devoted to a full development of human nature on all sides. This was superior in their view to the religious ideal of a human nature perfect on its moral side.

The Victorian preoccupation with the quest for certainty, made anxious by the cloud of doubt which obscured the light of Revelation, was not shared by the great agnostics, who showed and taught that it was possible to live confidently without certainty, since the only reliable opinions are those which are open to correction, and that assurance of certainty is a main source of evil, since it allows false opinions and bad institutions to remain and flourish. 'The beliefs which we have most warrant for have no safeguard to rest on, but a standing invitation to the whole world to prove them unfounded': this is the argument of the second chapter of Mill's essay, as it was the incessant argument of Huxley and others. Mill goes further in the remaining chapters and argues that the individual is entitled to live his private life in his own way on his own responsibility, free from the surveillance of moral police and from public inquisitorial rights. He saw the omnicompetence of the democratic State, the close organization of industrial society and the prestige and arrogance of democratic public opinion as a mounting threat to the individual, to man as his own end. In an earlier essay he had laid down that society absolutely required loyalty to 'something which is settled, something permanent, and not to be called in question; something which, by general agreement, has a right to be where it is, and to be secure against disturbance, whatever else may change.' He looked for this settled basis of society in 'the principles of individual freedom and political and social equality'. These are the principles of the open society.

Matthew Arnold's thinking, on the other hand, was emphasizing the role of the modern State in the 'humanization of man in society'. The social service State would draw into the public service, not least into education (in which Arnold himself served with devotion and distinction), the choicest spirits of the age who would devote their lives and their best thought as lovers of man's perfection to maintaining and improving the conditions of harmonious (all-sided) human development. Early in the century Bentham's principles – investigate, legislate, inspect – were systematically applied chiefly by his disciple Edwin Chadwick (1801–89), to all the great departments of public interest, and laid the foundations of the Welfare State. Supplementing this structural reorganization was the work of the Christian evangelicals who influenced legislation and who had pioneered with Wilberforce's agitation the form of voluntary association for social and humanitarian objects. The more recent consummation of all these tendencies is that the professions have been socialized and the social services professionalized.

The Tradition

With the great nineteenth-century agnostics, the 'apostles of culture' (and there are representative names in other countries) the humanist tradition is fully integrated and identified. They inherited the progressive ideals sloganized by the *philosophe* enlightenment – *reason, tolerance, humanity*; emancipation, *liberty, equality, fraternity*. They stood for standards of excellence in every field of achievement. They married science to 'poetry', democracy to culture, to produce harmonious all-round human development for all. They were agnostics, abandoning the quest for certainty and the orientation upon absolutes for reliable methods of progressive research, criticism, discussion, agreement. They enunciated the principles of the open society, a reconciliation of democratic social order and cooperation with the person as his own end. They saw these ideals institutionalized through the democratic procedures, the Welfare State, the social services and education. They linked their aspirations with the portrait in Thucydides of Periclean Athens and with the total achievement of the Greek genius. They wished to transcend cults and sects, parties and classes, and to universalize civilization as the humanization of man in society, and they believed that this was what they were doing.

The process of the humanist tradition integrated and identified in this outcome can be traced clearly. A key technical role is played by the successive classes of intellectuals – the sophists, the humanists, the virtuosi, the *philosophes*, the agnostics – who developed certain common disciplines or a common programme which changed the cultural climate in a strategic manner. Of these only the *philosophes* and the agnostics were fully concerned with social criticism and reconstruction and explicitly formulated humanist ideals – although many names belie this assertion, to mention only Protagoras, More, Locke.

How does this broad humanist tradition stand with regard to the sects: Platonists, Epicureans, Stoics, Churches, Positivists, Philosophical Radicals, Marxists, *et al.*? Only a detailed history can give a satisfactory answer. Broadly, however, it seems fair to say that Platonism, Stoicism and Christianity have made notable contributions, but that in spirit and essence all three are alien to the tradition, and by the time of the nineteenth-century agnostics the dominant strain is definitively humanist in the sense of agnostic or positivist and concentrated on man as his own end. Influences from these three sources began to be eclipsed in the seventeenth century. As for the other sects which may be termed 'humanist' in a narrower sense, they too have made notable and lasting contributions to the tradition, but they cannot claim to be its sole bearers. John Stuart Mill's celebrated essays on Bentham and Coleridge, and Mill in his own person, show that the rigid doctrines of a school cannot confine the human spirit of humanism. The most clearly defined surviving 'humanist' school, Marxism–Leninism, must be regarded as a deviant from the main humanist tradition because it is class-based, doctrinaire and 'metaphysical', opposed to the open mind and the open society, a system concerned with man rather than with men, the person as his own end. By contrast, some Christians share not only the earlier phases of the broad humanist tradition (as do the Marxists) but also some part of the last phase in which the tradition becomes specifically and definitively humanist in specifying the conditions and mutual relations of independence and interdependence, personal life and society. But Marxism–Leninism, having played its historical role, may rejoin the humanist tradition in the not remote future. Already, the theoreticians of Soviet atheism are using the word 'humanism' to express the interests of personal life.

However, the great humanist tradition is not best represented now nor likely to be handed on impressively by either the communists or the churches.

7

ORGANIZATION AND ACTIVITIES

Other Tributaries

ONE source of the humanist tradition not mentioned in the previous chapter was within the churches themselves. There were ancient and persistent heresies tending to modify Christian doctrine: Arianism doubted the divine nature of Christ; Pelagianism denied that mankind was infected with original sin. With the recovery at the Renaissance of Platonism, Stoicism and Epicureanism as ingredients in the discussion of human nature and destiny, tradition was enlarged and speculative thinking encouraged. Following the bitter religious intolerance and bloodshed of the sixteenth century and the use of violence in religious controversy, exemplified in Calvin's arguments with Castellio and Servetus which ended in the burning of the latter, there was a revulsion of feeling, a longing for a universal, rational and ethical religion and a repudiation of the jurisdiction of the civil power in religious questions. These feelings created a new ethos of religious thought in the late seventeenth century.

Locke, who was a spokesman of the age on so many other issues, expressed also this theme in his *A Letter Concerning Toleration* published in Latin in Holland in 1685. For Locke was touched by all the streams of liberal influence of the time. He was intimate with the Cambridge Platonists and he knew and lived with in exile in Holland all kinds of refugees fleeing from intolerant churches and regimes. The *Letter* opens with the statement that if anyone is 'destitute of charity, meekness, and good-will in general towards all mankind, even to those who are not Christians, he is certainly yet short of being a true Christian himself'. Thus Christianity is itself the teaching and preaching of toleration. Moreover, no power on earth can take away from any man his own personal responsibility for finding out what he ought to believe and how he ought to live: 'No way whatsoever that I shall walk in against the dictates of my conscience will ever bring me to the mansions of the blessed.' In a Postscript, Locke repeats an old argument that since the Bible is the sole rule of faith for Protestant Christians, only doctrines in the express words of Scripture about which there can be no question are fundamental and required. All alleged deductions from or elaborations compatible with biblical teaching are merely human teaching liable to be infected with human arrogance.

Locke's English translator and friend was a Unitarian or Socinian. These were the most radical of dissenters (and Arians), who went furthest in playing down dogma and playing up conduct. If the Bible is the sole rule of faith, and if in his reading and understanding of the Bible a man is to be guided solely by his reason and conscience, no received doctrine of the church can stand which offends our common sense or our moral sense. This was a sufficient ground for the rejection of the doctrines of Original Sin, the Atonement, Justification by faith, Predestination, the Trinity and everlasting punishment. In a word, the whole scheme of Christian salvation was jettisoned, and the small craft sailed on boldly piloted by the lone hand, steering by the uncontrovertible ethical texts of Scripture which regulated men's lives 'according to the rules of virtue and piety'. This trust in reason and individualism as the road to unity which dogmatism and authoritarianism had failed to gain was not justified, if only because dogmatism and authoritarianism barred the way. But it was the Socinians (become Unitarians) among all the Dissenters who pre-eminently attacked with vigour the forces of dogmatism and authoritarianism that remained entrenched. The names of Richard Price and Joseph Priestley, Unitarians educated in Dissenting Academies, are high among the opponents of Burke and militant champions of the revolutionary democrats of America and France. The spear-head of the Dissenters are found attacking on the political front in the eighteenth century. The tumultuous and proliferating sects of the early seventeenth century had died down or died out. The survivors became respectable because more or less orthodox or carried forward the old cause of freedom of conscience into the new cause of liberty and democracy.

This strong blend of religious and political radicalism was well represented in South Place Chapel, Finsbury, under its minister William Johnson Fox (1786–1864), who became one of the most notable orators of the day in the Corn Law agitation and a leader-writer in radical newspapers. The orientation he gave to South Place was untrammelled freedom of inquiry. The minister and his congregation expected themselves and expected their successors to learn and grow: their primary allegiance was to virtue and freedom, and they did not bind themselves by dogmas. John Stuart Mill said of him: 'Fox's religion was what the religion of all would be if we were in a healthy state; a religion of spirit not of dogma, and catholic in the best sense.' To religion of this temper was joined a passionate interest in popular education and in public affairs and social reform. The minister was not theologian and preacher, but reformer and publicist. Fox's successor Moncure Conway carried on and developed in his own way this cultural tradition, and today South Place, now South Place Ethical Society, is still a platform for responsible outspoken thought that is no respecter of persons, still less of sects.

In the intellectual storms of the nineteenth century congregations broke from theological moorings. When the critical philosophy of Hume and Kant had done its work natural theology was in ruins. Darwin's theory opened up a new line of thought, and indeed provided a new bible, and the critical work on the old Bible destroyed the claim of an infallible revelation. This all-round unsettlement involved many churches and congregations, some of which emerged from the heavy seas of doubt and difficulty into a kind of religious humanism which had left behind even the worship of a supreme being. Religious myths and symbols were given the validity of poetry; absolute ideals (Truth, Beauty, Goodness) took the place of God as the real object of attention and devotion. 'Free congregations' following this course separated from the orthodox churches in Germany, both Catholic and Protestant, in the later nineteenth century.

The Ethical Movement

An independent development was the foundation of Ethical Societies in the last decades of the century, since these were new foundations and not existing congregations – save in the case of South Place which adopted the name at the instance of Stanton Coit when he became their minister and was at the same time helping to form the Ethical Societies. Stanton Coit came from America, like Conway before him, as a colleague of Felix Adler who had founded the Society for Ethical Culture in New York in 1876. Adler was the son of a leading Rabbi and destined for the ministry, but lost the faith of his fathers during the course of his higher education in Germany. When he returned to New York he was induced to form an association based on 'the autonomy of ethics', the moral responsibility of the individual for his life. He welcomed into his movement pure secularists who shared this standpoint as well as religiously minded people. Adler founded also in connexion with the Society an important progressive school, and the Society won respect in New York for its pioneer social work. Following his example, others formed Ethical Societies in other American cities and in Europe. The idea was brought to England by Coit and others, and interested particularly teachers of moral philosophy in the universities and in general those who felt that social reform and socialism needed to be grounded in permanent and examined principles of action and to lay hold of criticized values and ends. There was a group at the time with similar ideas calling itself the 'Fellowship of the New Life'. Influences from different quarters brought into existence out of the membership of this group the Fabian Society and the London Ethical Society. The Fabians were the heirs of the Philosophical Radicals. The Ethical Movement was perhaps more of a break with the past and a new beginning.

The main purpose of the Ethical Societies was to disentangle moral ideals from religious doctrines, metaphysical systems and ethical theories, and to make them an independent force in personal life and social relations. The stress on the independence and importance of ethical principles and on the impossibility of substituting religious dependence for moral self-dependence (each one his own authority for his own judgements and acts) was not intended to be an attack on the churches nor competition with them, but rather to establish an ethical foundation for social reform and an ethical outlook to survive the decay of religious conviction. The Ethical Societies were supported by moral philosophers of different schools. Adler himself had been profoundly influenced by Kant, whose practical imperative was a fundamental humanism: 'Act so as to use humanity, whether in your own person or in the person of another, always as an end, never as merely a means.' Henry Sidgwick, the most distinguished, who formed the Cambridge Ethical Society, was still a Utilitarian. Borrowing a phrase from Bacon, he said the Ethical Societies provided a platform for the discussion of 'middle axioms' and their application to present problems. There was an ethical agnosticism or positivism comparable with scientific agnosticism or positivism. Scientific agnosticism ignored metaphysical questions and got on with the job of building up positive knowledge. Ethical agnosticism ignored questions of ethical theory and got on with the job of rousing people to make and discuss and act on moral judgements because this was their inescapable responsibility, and that responsibility was their main certitude and the starting-point of every personal life.

The Ethical Movement was thus involved in programmes of moral education in State schools, in penal reform, in settlement and neighbourhood community work, in assisting the women's movement, in promoting attention to racial, colonial and international problems. In all these and in other fields the movement initiated or supported effective action. Moreover, the movement both enlisted the help of leading men and women in progressive causes and encouraged and inspired its own members to engage in public service through politics or through voluntary associations for public ends. In 1896 the Ethical Societies in England formed a Union, which was incorporated in 1928 as The Ethical Union. An International Ethical Union was formed in Zurich in 1896. A quarterly, the *International Journal of Ethics*, had been started in 1890.

The Rationalist Press Association

Behind the inaugural meeting of the RPA in the rooms of the Ethical Union in 1899 lay half a century of freethought and secularist propaganda and agitation, led principally by Charles Bradlaugh, who had founded the National Secular Society in 1866 and the weekly journal *The National Reformer*, and George Jacob Holyoake, a founder of the Cooperative Movement. Charles Albert Watts had worked on *The National Reformer* and he was the organizing genius who brought together the men and got the backing to launch the RPA. The venture was a pioneer book club and paperback publishing house, with a publisher's circular, *The Literary Guide*, developed as a monthly magazine. Watts had already issued the *Agnostic Annual* in 1884, which later appeared as the *Rationalist Annual*. The RPA eventually sold books by the million through C. A. Watts & Co. The outstanding success was 'The Thinker's Library' inaugurated by F. C. C. Watts in 1929, which exploited the earlier policy of cheap reprints and added many new titles on subjects of interest to the scientifically minded. Natural science and biblical criticism had been the two staple interests from the start, but the establishment of biblical criticism as a regular theological discipline left little to be done in this field, and Sir Allen Lane's Penguin coup practically obliterated the earlier venture in paperback publishing.

The Rationalist Press Association, the Ethical Union, South Place Ethical Society, and the National Secular Society were related organizations, well known to each other, with overlapping memberships and frequent contacts, but independent in origins and different in functions. There were also differences of temperament and emphasis, and indeed of interest and outlook. In these first decades of the century the word 'humanist' was sometimes used to describe the 'rationalist–ethical' outlook, particularly in the Ethical Union, whose journal was for a time called *The Humanist*.

The International

The Second World War broke the World Union of Free-thinkers, and the International Ethical Union had already declined. The Ethical Union, after some explorations with surviving elements of the World Union of Freethinkers, took the initiative with the Dutch Humanist League in calling a Congress in Amsterdam in 1952 which inaugurated the International Humanist and Ethical Union. Sir Julian Huxley presided at the Congress, and the founding members were the Dutch Humanist League, the Belgian Humanist League, the British Ethical Union, the American Ethical Union, the American Humanist Association and the Indian Radical Humanist Movement. Thus the Ethical Societies of the 1870s found themselves together with some post-war humanist movements and able to unite in a common declaration and a common organization. The Dutch and Belgian movements had sprung up from the confessional soil of Holland and Flemish-speaking Belgium after the experience of the German occupation, when those who were not in any of the churches found themselves morally isolated. Their felt need for their own form of moral solidarity made them responsive to the initiatives of Dr J. P. van Praag and Dr J. in't Veld by whom was formed in 1945 Humanitas, an association for social work, and in 1946 the Humanistisch Verbond. The League vigorously asserted itself and by its exertions obtained equal legal and social recognition with the churches. Although a new post-war development, the Dutch Humanist League represented and embodied an important tradition in Dutch history.

The American Humanist Association was the outcome of a 'Humanist Manifesto' published in 1933 with the signatures of more than thirty well-known philosophers and ministers of liberal churches. Following this initiative an organized association was formed in 1949 with a journal *The Humanist*. The Indian movement had a political, not a religious, background. Its founder M. N. Roy had been one of the leaders of the Congress Party, of comparable stature with Nehru. As a young man he had been called by Lenin to serve on the Comintern and had been sent with Bukharin to China to report back on the situation there. He became convinced that freedom was the essence of man's nature, and broke with Lenin and with Marxism. Returning to India, he was gaoled by the British and spent six years in prison writing voluminously. Reading his two volumes *Reason, Romanticism, and Revolution*, one feels one is meeting again the passionate intelligence of Condorcet or one of the *philosophes*. Indeed, Roy wanted for India a Renaissance and an Enlightenment. When the war came he took the most unpopular line a Congress leader could take: he sided with the British against Gandhi because he believed that Nazism was the most evil thing on earth which had to be opposed by all means. He seceded with his own followers from the Congress Party and formed an independent Radical Democratic Party, which he soon turned into a Radical Humanist Movement to work for the political and cultural education of the peoples of India, that is, for enlightenment and emancipation.

These founding members, with the remnant of the old Ethical Society of Vienna which had a proud record of uncompromising free speech and liberal principles until Hitler entered Vienna and sent the two leaders to a concentration camp, brought into existence IHEU in Amsterdam in 1952. Since then, Congresses have been held in London, Oslo and Paris. A large German movement, the Bund Freireligiöser Gemeinden Deutschlands, a federation of the old 'free congregations', and a still larger old-established French movement, La Ligue Française de l'Enseignement, have joined, together with new groups in Norway, Italy, Denmark, Japan, South Korea, Australia, Argentina, Canada, the Philippines, Nigeria. IHEU can be said to include all organized humanist movements throughout the world. The secretariat is in Utrecht, where a quarterly is published, *International Humanism*. IHEU is a recognized Non-governmental Organization with the UN and with UNESCO. All its member-organizations are steadily expanding.

The tradition created by the sophists, the humanists, the

virtuosi, the *philosophes* and the agnostics is a general inheritance, not the possession of a sect or sects like the tradition of dissent. But a dissenting chapel like South Place broke the bonds and crossed the borders of sectarianism into this open tradition. Similarly, the Ethical Union with its ethical positivism and strong interest in freedom of conscience, political liberty and social reform, and the RPA with its scientific positivism and practical endeavour to give effect to freedom of inquiry and information were organized forms of the open tradition, working as a leaven, not new sects. Thus the humanist organizations united in IHEU cannot claim exclusive possession of the broad humanist tradition which permeates Western civilization, for this would be absurd, but they may claim to represent and embody that tradition in a uniquely conscious and purposeful way. They have the will to make it their own and to make it prevail, to bring together scientific positivism and ethical positivism, radical politics and the arts and humanities, for the plenitude of human development and the fulfilment of all.

British Humanist Association

In 1963 the Ethical Union joined with the RPA to form the British Humanist Association. *The Literary Guide* had been changed to *The Humanist*. 'Humanism' was increasingly used to identify a certain outlook, not least by churchmen, and had come to stand for something in the public mind. An inaugural dinner was held in the House of Commons in May 1963 with Sir Julian Huxley, the first president, in the chair. There was an immediate response, and a steady accession of members strengthened local groups affiliated in the EU and formed new local humanist groups. About the same time, Humanist Groups which had been formed in the universities were brought together and instituted the University Humanist Federation. In 1965 the EU was removed from the register of charities on a technical point, which necessitated the withdrawal of the charitable RPA. The outcome was settled by an extraordinary general meeting of the Ethical Union in January

1967 which changed the name to British Humanist Association.

The British Humanist Association exists to spread humanist ideas and ideals, to cultivate the understanding and application of them, to defend them and their adherents from misrepresentation and discrimination, to form fellowships for mutual support and common action, to help to educate its members in living, and to help them to raise the quality and the value of life. This work is carried out through publications, courses and conferences, local and special groups, social projects, a counselling service, political action. It remains to indicate concretely the character and scope of this work and its further possibilities, which can conveniently be considered under the heads: propaganda, groups, courses and conferences, counselling, projects, political action, rituals.

Propaganda

A humanist literature is growing. At least two bibliographies have been published which list hundreds of titles. Most of these books are not produced or sponsored by organized humanists, though some are, but they can be recognized, reviewed and recommended in humanist journals. The RPA publish a monthly magazine *Humanist* and *Question*, a miscellany which is issued once or twice a year. They publish also through a subsidiary 'The Humanist Library' which has one or two new titles each year. The BHA publishes monthly *Humanist News*. South Place Ethical Society has its own monthly journal *The Ethical Record* which regularly carries full summaries of all the lectures delivered on Sunday mornings. Leading humanists connected with the movement have been and are prolific authors. Notably, Sir Julian Huxley organized a symposium *The Humanist Frame* published in 1961, designed to bring together the thinking of leading humanists in a wide diversity of the arts and sciences. Professor A. J. Ayer, second president of the British Humanist Association, edited a similar collection of essays, *The Humanist Outlook*, contributed by members of the Advisory Council of the BHA and published in 1968. In this abundant and growing literature, humanism acquires depth and variety of appeal and develops an adequacy to human needs and experience. The explicitly humanist literature created since the eighteenth century is already a monumental witness to the vitality and validity and ineffaceable permanence of these ideas and ideals.

This being so, it is a wonder that humanists have some difficulty in broadcasting their ideas and ideals. The churches are entrenched in broadcasting and produce regular programmes. Humanists have no regular opportunity of the same kind, no recognized constituency. This is extraordinary, and will seem incredible to posterity. They order things differently abroad.

Humanist Groups

The local humanist group is first of all a fellowship of like-minded persons who meet to find out what others of their own mind think and to reflect again on what they think themselves. The early discussions of the group help its members to become more clearly and critically aware of what they believe and what they want. In learning this they may also develop bonds with the group, and the group may develop an identity. Unless a group does establish itself in this way as of value and valued, like a friendship, it is not likely to persist and develop.

The thriving group turns outwards, perhaps in the second phase of its development, to the neighbourhood. Perhaps after a systematic survey of what is there and what is going on, the group sees what is amiss or what is missing, and where it comes in. The group tries to bear its share of community care, to cooperate with other groups in public service, and to initiate projects that will bring new benefits or opportunities to the life of the neighbourhood.

A humanist group does not exist for the exclusive benefit of its members, like a tennis club, for its humanism involves an acceptance of a share of responsibility for the conditions of human life. That begins at home with face-to-face contacts and first-hand experience, but it should not end there. Ideally, the group should also take an active interest in some aspect of national affairs and bear some share of responsibility for meeting the needs of peoples overseas in the developing parts of the world. To be in this way in responsive touch on three fronts with the reality of human conditions is practical humanism. If the group initiates and maintains activities on these fronts, the individual humanist is stimulated and enabled to play his part and to do more than he would otherwise be likely to do to fulfil effectively the obligations of his humanism. The group also may and should engage in the propagation of humanism in which it believes, but unless the humanism it propagates begets this kind of service it is not breeding true.

The question may be asked: is this practical humanism not merely a secular imitation of Christian charitable work and Christian missions? The answer is that in so far as Christian charitable work is done for its own sake as a human obligation to better human conditions it is indistinguishable from practical humanism. Our membership one of another is a more binding allegiance than membership of any sect or group, and humanism makes no sense if it is not identified with the social conscience which acknowledges this allegiance. If Christian faith died out and Christian inspiration and incentives were lost to the world, human social obligations would not be diminished. Humanism is an unqualified acceptance of these obligations. The justification? In the long term, these are the conditions on which life on humanist assumptions is judged worth living.

In addition to local groups, some special groups are formed for a specific purpose or for a particular interest. For example, a Humanist Teachers Association was formed because a high proportion of the members of the BHA are teachers and because humanist teachers have special problems and concerns. A Working Party for Social Action has responsibility for encouraging and helping humanists to take social action in the community.

The BHA Education Committee, which includes some leading educators, is mainly concerned with policy and action on moral education. This has been a subject of special and continuing concern within the movement. In 1897 the Union of Ethical Societies formed a Moral Instruction League which in the period before the First World War made a strong impact on public policy and educational practice. The League's *Syllabus* was widely adopted by LEAs and was endorsed by the President of the Board of Education in a debate in the House in 1909 on a motion moved on behalf of the League by Dr G. P. Gooch. The League organized demonstration lessons for teachers and parents and training college staff, and produced manuals. In 1907 the Union of Ethical Societies founded the Secular Education League.

After the Education Act of 1944, secular education as a political issue was dead and the approach of the old Moral Instruction League was outmoded. (Indeed, before it was wound up it had become the Civic Education League.) But the issues remained, and remain. Compulsory religion in the county schools, even with the provision for exemption and with no religious tests for teachers, has proved gravely unsatisfactory to many, including Christians who want their religion in the schools. There are three unsatisfactory elements: 1. Underlying the compulsory act of worship at the daily morning assembly of the school is the assumption that the school is or ought to be a Christian community because the nation at large is a Christian people. This assumption is so far at variance with the facts as known to children and staff that the pretence is a hollow mockery. 2. Parents who are humanists are put in a difficult position, since they have the dilemma of allowing their children to be treated as Christians or exposing them to the hazards of segregation. 3. Staff who are humanists are put in an even more difficult position, since they are tempted to conform for the sake of the Head or of the school or of their own prospects of promotion. The practice of religion in county schools under the Act thus tends to be corrupting, and is equally damaging to religious and to educational ideals.

Leading humanists and Christians concerned with education formed an unofficial group to discuss this situation who

met over a period of eighteen months and issued a joint statement in the form of a pamphlet 'Religious and Moral Education in County Schools'. This statement advocated an 'open'
approach to the teaching and practice of religion at all stages
in the county schools. Christianity so long as it remained
privileged in the school curriculum was not to be protected
and the child was to be protected – from indoctrination.
Religious education should be education in and for choice.
Therefore alternatives to Christianity should be acknowledged
within the school as real and respectable. The group suggested
that the act of worship need not be daily but might be perhaps
twice a week, so that alternative forms of assembly might be
tried, and so that the Head might be able to meet the school in
assembly uncomplicated by an act of worship involving
personal beliefs.

Some 10,000 copies of the pamphlet were bought by
Colleges of Education and LEAs and others for discussion,
and evidence showed that the recommendations of the group
were having a liberal influence. Nevertheless, a majority of the
Humanist Teachers Association disliked and repudiated the
pamphlet as a weak compromise. In particular, they could not
tolerate that the Christian faith should be taught in the county
schools as true, even if challenged, nor that an official act of
worship should be compulsorily required, nor that moral
education should be in any way bound up with religious
teaching. These were matters on which they felt they could
not be party to any compromise. In 1967 the Annual General
Meeting of the BHA adopted a statement of position prepared
by the Education Committee, which summarized humanist
objections to present regulations and accepted the task of
gaining the support of parents and teachers for the changes
proposed.

Courses and Conferences

Regular one-day courses for inquirers and new members are
held in London, and several week-end courses are arranged
each year in different parts of the country, many of them in the

programmes of county adult education colleges. Typical subjects of the courses have been: 'Fact and Value', 'The Open Society', 'Ideas of Human Nature', 'Morals with and without Religion', 'Human Relationships as a Basis for Morality', 'Humanism and the Arts', 'The Humanist Tradition'. When appropriate, Christian lecturers are invited to join the tutorial staff for the course, which in any case usually includes a number of non-humanists.

The annual conference of the BHA and the annual conference of the UHF are usually concerned with questions of the day. Subjects of the BHA conferences have been: 'Youth in Revolt?', 'Co-existence of East and West', 'The Scientific Revolution', 'Reappraisals of the Family', 'Aggression'. The UHF have taken as subjects for their conferences: 'A Humanist Approach to Social and Political Problems', 'Education', 'Marriage and the Place of Women in Society', 'Crime and Punishment', 'Modern Youth'.

The courses and conferences are designed to stimulate and inform the thinking of humanists on central questions of permanent importance and on questions of the day, and to introduce others to humanist thinking. They also provide social occasions for humanists to meet one another outside their local group, if they belong to one. For this purpose also humanist holidays at home and abroad have been arranged.

Counselling

The title of one week-end course was 'Mental Health: a Humanist Concern'. Greek therapeutic moral philosophies like Stoicism and Epicureanism aimed at serenity as the goal of self-management. Immunity from disturbance, an absolute inner security, is hardly a feasible nor even a desirable modern ideal. But one needs to be able to cope with stress, to be enabled to deal with distress, and to avoid breakdown. Many require help at some time and perhaps all would benefit by it. We should help each other, and particularly those who share the same premises for the lives they live should help each other. But help requires help, for it is easier to do harm than good. To tell another what one thinks, to give good advice, to prescribe what to do is not the helping hand but the inconsiderate push. The distressed mind is ill and needs professional help, but people can be helped to cope with stresses and strains by others who are skilled in first-aid and preventive work. The disparity between ambition and reality, maladjustment in a job or in a personal relationship, the burden of an exacting and half-acknowledged duty, sexual frustration: these and like sources of a persistent malaise or unhappiness may often be faced squarely and dealt with adequately out of the person's own resources with well-directed outside help. Self-dependence, acknowledged interdependence and dependability, taken together are strong indications of mental health. The counsellor, acting upon an acknowledged interdependence, is helping the person counselled to gain or to regain due self-dependence and dependability.

The Dutch Humanist League from the beginning developed a counselling service for its own members and available outside to 'non-confessional' people, especially in hospitals, prisons and the armed forces. They have now some 700 trained volunteers and ten full-time organizers of the service. The BHA held its first training course in 1964, and a service was announced as available at the end of 1965. Humanist organizations in other countries have developed services of this kind, and it can be said that 'counselling' is a recognized part of organized humanism, for it is the most practical part of education in living.

Mental health is probably liable to greater hazards than physical health. Man's picture of his world is liable to be seriously distorted very early by stresses and conflicts represented in the inner world of phantasy, and the distortion is liable to be reinforced by later interpretations and experiences. Humanism as a sustained attempt to live with reality cannot be limited to giving a rational picture of the world in general terms; it must go on to help the individual to live in that world by dealing realistically with his own inadequate ill-adapted responses.

The function of humanist counsellors includes not only counselling those who seek their help, but also leading discussions on personal problems, and visiting prisons, hospitals, old persons, and others in situations of isolation and stress. The preparation for this begins with the formation of a small group of volunteers for counselling who meet regularly with someone professionally qualified. After an initial period of professional guidance, the counsellors continue to meet regularly to discuss case 'material' out of their own experience, to acquire from outside specialists knowledge of the work of relevant special services available to help people in difficulty, and to perfect their integration as a group. The maintenance of the group, meeting loyally and regularly, is a *sine qua non* of an effective counselling service. The group gives its members resources and a confidence greater than they have, and an experience of lived equality and interdependence, stripped of all pretences and pretensions, which is an invaluable and necessary preparation for the counselling situation. This discipline also enables the counsellors to assume corporate responsibility for the maintenance, expansion and control of the counselling service, upholding its outlook and standards.

A main target of training courses in counselling is to have one or two trained counsellors in every local humanist group. Their function in the group would be not only to undertake local counselling work and to train volunteers for local visiting, but also to leaven the group as a group with the 'counselling approach', that is, a relaxed, disarmed, forthcoming, candid response to fellow members, an acceptance of equality, a readiness to help and to be helped on all matters of humanist thinking and conduct. Having experienced the discipline of the counselling group, the counsellor will also perhaps be inspired and enabled to achieve a similar integration and creative power in the local group or in a nucleus within the group. The group is not primarily a therapeutic group; it is a purposive group and a group of like-minded friends. The purposiveness, like-mindedness and friendship need to be cultivated so that they fertilize each other in a productive way. This tends to happen but does not happen inevitably, and the counsellor's intensive experience of the counselling group helps to make it happen. For this is a liberating experience of great value, an experience of the reality and the meaning of human equality and interdependence and independence.

'Counselling' permeates our Western culture, if the word is taken to mean an informed and skilled help which tries to reduce suffering and inadequacy in all situations by using the skill to share the information. Applied psychology and applied sociology are transforming human existence in a new way, mainly through the social services, so that it can be said that the 'counsellors' (primarily the professionals) have the key role in the present phase of development which in the Western humanist tradition has been played successively by the sophists, the humanists, the virtuosi, the *philosophes*, and the agnostics. The 'counsellors' have particular technical roles in the complex of social services they staff, but as a class, like their predecessors, they are creating a new cultural climate, and like their predecessors they are striving to live and to help others to live in the light of modern knowledge. As always, this is a challenge to traditional ideas and ideals.

Projects

The main principle of all humanist counselling and social work – and education – must be the reciprocal formula: self-dependence and dependability based on interdependence. The individuals, the group, the people being helped must be enabled to stand on their own feet, see things for themselves, make their own judgements and decisions, choose their own values, because from the outset their initiatives are stimulated and their cooperation enlisted. This was the principle of the 'Socratic' method of discussion, perhaps invented by the first and greatest of the sophists, Protagoras; and it was the principle invoked by Pericles in the famous speech in Thucydides in the passage in which he said that ordinary citizens who took no part in public affairs were regarded not as unambitious but as useless, and went on: 'we Athenians are able to judge at all events if we cannot originate, and instead of looking on discussion as a stumbling-block in the way of action, we think it an indispensable preliminary to any wise action at all.'

In our own day, Danilo Dolci, working in Sicily amongst a people singularly lacking in interdependence and dependability, mutually suspicious and hostile, apathetic and withdrawn, narrow, unforthcoming and unprogressive, has induced and cultivated the beginnings of a changing pattern of human relations and a changing outlook on human possibilities mainly by discussion meetings in which people express and examine their own attitudes and opinions and those of others in the group, and are led into mutual consultation, the planning of developments with technical help, and the sustained cooperation required to go through with a project. Similarly, in a different context, another good humanist, Richard Hauser, has employed his own shock tactics with tough, rejected or despaired-of elements in our own society, taking them unawares and getting under their guard, their protective devices and entrenched resistances, so that they become surprisingly aware of their own creative possibilities and of the needs of others to which they can make an effective response. They are helped by being enabled to help. In this way the 'peer group' is stirred up to deal with its own problem; no 'solution' is offered from outside. Bored suburban housewives get together about their situation. Juvenile delinquents tackle juvenile delinquency.*

In England the local humanist group is encouraged and expected to work on these lines, activating mutual aid and public service as much as dispensing benefits. In such ways the services and institutions of a Welfare State are being translated into the full mutuality of a welfare society. The key role is played by the 'counsellors' in the extended sense who are 'representative', showing what is normally required of ordinary citizens in everyday human relations in our modern cooperative and productive societies. The total ideal is an

---

*Danilo Dolci: *Waste*, Trans. R. Munroe, London, 1963. R. & H. Hauser: *The Fraternal Society*, London, 1962.

acknowledged interdependence and an acknowledged independence, sustained by normal self-dependence and dependability.

Abroad, the humanist movement follows the same line and is interested in initiating and supporting development schemes based on these principles. A brilliant example, pioneered by Patrick van Rensburg and his wife, is Swaneng Hill School, which was the first non-racial, co-educational secondary school in Bechuanaland, largely built by the pupils and rapidly expanded by voluntary help and aid from all quarters. The self-help is reflected in the cost of about £200 a place compared with about £550 in Zambia's new secondary schools. Moreover, the self-help principle is inculcated in the educational programme, and the school has become a pioneered base for pioneer development in the district and in the newly independent Botswana.

Similarly, when the Freedom from Hunger Campaign was inaugurated by FAO, at the request of IHEU the Radical Humanist Movement in India initiated a development project in Bihar with the help of one of their members, Shiopujan Singh Shastri, supported by a local group of the IRHM. The main feature of the scheme is that with the balanced assistance of local, government and overseas resources a planned attempt is being made, based on full local consultations and discussions, to bring every element of the population into a programme of development which will itself achieve self-dependence and provide conditions of self-dependence for all.

Humanists in Britain have formed a Housing Association which has completed two exemplary projects for housing elderly persons, and is engaged on a third. At the other end of the age-range, an Agnostics Adoption Society was formed to help responsible and suitable would-be adoptive parents who do not profess a religious belief and cannot undertake to bring up a child in a religious faith. The Edinburgh Humanist Society has opened a Youth Home for boys. In such ways organized humanism makes a modest but increasing contribution according to its resources to 'community care'.

Politics

The Greeks laid the foundations of humanism with their concentrated attention upon the 'examined' life and the 'good' life. The 'examined' life led to their inquiry into truth and justice, the 'good' life to their concern with education and politics. The conditions of men's life together which settled the possibilities for each one were settled in the 'city'. The 'good' life was bound up with the 'city'. If organized humanism is concerned first and last with obtaining for all the conditions of a life worthy to be called human it is concerned with politics, with the decisions and policies which go so far to determine these conditions. Bentham argued that of all human evils misgovernment is the most calamitous, since it is irresistible, for it turns against men the very instrument of their security and the condition of self-help. Organized humanism is inseparable from the open society. Without the security and basic forms of cooperation established in an open society, and some corresponding form of world order, humanist values and humanist programmes of education in living exist under threat; the ground for confidence in them is undermined.

These basic conditions, within the 'city' and throughout the world, are therefore the primary concern of humanist politics. A humanist movement may decide to support a particular political programme or to work with a particular political party at a particular time, or to support and work with a particular lobby or pressure group, but it is not itself a political party nor a particular pressure group. All the same, it would be absurd to stand and work for the open society and a world order and not be interested and engaged in 'politics', not want and hope to influence public decisions and policies which make the conditions of men's life together. Having said this, it would be logical to go on to list the reforms and policies organized humanists try to promote and the pressure groups they actually support, but the methods and objects of humanist political action belong to the larger body of considerations that will be dealt with in the chapter 'Strategy and Tactics'.

Rituals

If in a broad sense 'religion' is taken to mean an inner world of personal belief and response and 'politics' an outer world of regulated conditions of a common life, 'ritual' is an intersection where a personal event takes place in a social context. Birth, marriage and death are private events of moment which have this public face. They call for publicity, solemnity, celebration, public participation. They take people through the church doors who otherwise never go near the church. If organized humanism offers an alternative to traditional religion what is done about these occasions which are felt to be socially important, as they are personally important?

Obviously, christening, baptism, confirmation imply not merely the political society and the sustaining community but mainly a body of believers and their faith in which the child is to be brought up or which he decisively adopts for himself. If the political society and the community of believers are not identical, the ritual becomes exclusively religious. The society as such is not represented and does not participate. When unbelievers resort to the church on these occasions they may be asking for social participation in their private event. Organized humanists can offer their members the sanction and support of their own 'community' on these occasions. Indeed, 'naming ceremonies' have been devised and performed, and there is no particular difficulty about doing this worthily and acceptably, but in such ceremonies the humanist organization will try to represent the responsible society rather than a particular sect. This is seen clearly in the case of the Norwegian humanist organization which developed out of an initiative to institute a form of civic confirmation for unbelieving adolescents. Following a course of instruction, the young people formally assumed their civic responsibilities at a ceremony in the town-hall of Oslo, with the participation of civic dignitaries and the city orchestra.

Civil marriages in England have an official ritual. They take place in a register office in the presence of the registrar and 'two or more credible witnesses' and a 'Solemn Declaration and Contracting Words' are spoken by both parties. Under the Marriage Acts, apart from Anglican churches and register offices, a marriage can be solemnized only in places of worship registered for the purpose, except that special provisions have been made for Jews and members of the Society of Friends. Thus humanists who feel that the official ritual in the register office is bleak or inadequate have no alternative, unless they are prepared to go to church and the minister of the church is prepared to overlook their having no possible part in his community. Official humanist policy has not been to try to obtain special provision such as has been allowed to Jews and members of the Society of Friends, but to encourage local groups of humanists to investigate the facilities and practices in their own areas, and to press the responsible local authorities for improvements where the standards are not good enough. In conformity with their other policies, humanists want to raise the general standard of the social service for all even in this public participation in a private event.

However, this may be a mistaken idea. Maybe these private events should be ritualized by independent like-minded groups to which people belong, and not by or on behalf of the whole society. Perhaps they belong to the private sector and not the public sector of the open society.

For the bereaved, death may be the most fearful personal event of all, the hardest to come to terms with and accept and survive effectively. This is the private event which may most urgently call for and most resistingly shun public participation. Geoffrey Gorer (*Death, Grief, and Mourning in Contemporary Britain*, 1965) has expressed the view that the modern tendency to cut out mourning and the public acknowledgement of grief often seriously damages the bereaved and prevents a proper recovery. Here membership in a group beyond the family may really help, if the group knows how to help, and this is a function that can be learned like any other. The funeral rite itself can be treated in different ways: nothing at all; music only; simple words spoken or read, with or without music; the tributes of friends. Usually on such occasions relatives and friends gather together afterwards at the house or elsewhere. This gathering of friends and relatives might be divorced from disposal of the body (which can be cremated without ceremony) and made a memorial meeting which recalls to life the dead in the recollections of his friends, so that he is not dispersed in unspoken thoughts but is reaffirmed and repossessed in a collective act which establishes the image of his identity and quality with its own power of self-perpetuation in the memories and lives of others. This is a harvest ritual, not a tomb ritual, not a process of mourning but of fulfilment, a realization of value not a recognition of pointlessness, of achievement and permanence not of futility and ephemerality. What if the realism is too keen, if the dead, and their friends, cannot stand the test of the humanist response to death? Sometimes it may be better to draw the curtain, but most often there is grain to be winnowed.

Although the ritualization of personal events may properly belong to the private sector, the ritualization of public events is a public act; but in an open society the public act should not be a religious rite. Elsewhere I have suggested an annual world-wide celebration of UN Day as a needed new universal ritual. Humanists would like to see whatever social rituals are needed dissociated from particular religious rites so that they may be universally shared.

*

The organization and activities characteristic of a humanist movement offer the individual humanist a flexible instrument adaptable to social change by which he can make his humanism effective. Mediating between the helpless individual and an impersonal highly organized world of power and trends, the movement promises to become more effective in humanizing that world as it draws in more members. Learning to know the conditions of living well and the difficulties of living well, ready to take help and to give help, recognizing how relative any success really is, every humanist on his way to becoming a person with a life of his own finds his power and his significance vastly enhanced by the capabilities which the movement develops.

8

FRIENDS AND ENEMIES

What is tolerance? it is the consequence of humanity.
We are all formed of frailty and error; let us pardon
reciprocally each other's folly.

Voltaire

The antagonism between the ideal and the actual, the
spiritual and the natural, is the source of the deepest
and most injurious of all enmities.

John Dewey

Discriminations

WHO is the enemy? Declare whom you are against, and we
shall know who you are. A man is known by the company he
keeps – and avoids.

Let me, then, begin by saying that I love and venerate Voltaire and Diderot, David Hume and Charles James Fox, to
re-open only one chapter of human affairs, that I respond unreservedly to their humanity in which I feel consoled, raised,
invigorated and reassured. And let me go on to say that I not
only abhor the Napoleons of this world but also am repelled by
St Francis, at the head of a bead-roll of saints in whom I feel
my own humanity chilled, alienated, depressed, deflated, impoverished. The sublimated love of the saints, holy charity,
the grace of God manifested in the rapture and passion of the
self-surrendered soul in whom Christ reigns seems to me a thin
and shrill version of our nature compared with the genial
humanity of a generous person. Humanity rather than spiritu-
ality I find admirable, and I find it in the Reverend Sidney
Smith rather than in the Reverend John Henry Newman.

This personal naming may seem to many the most revealing
thing so far, a practical confession of faith, a concrete expression of ideals and values which does more to expose humanism
than any argument because it points to what can be bio-
graphically known and compared if not actually seen. To stand
with Freud against Kierkegaard, with Montaigne against

Luther, not merely on their side of the argument but mainly with them as human beings is to be identified at the deepest level of personal identity, where one gives oneself away unreservedly with an impulse reinforced by reflection. This is what I essentially am because this is where I belong in aspiration. Here I am judged by the company I keep and the company I avoid, because it is self-identification.

Are humanists, then, those who prefer Socrates to Christ? Symbolically, perhaps this is so, but to insist that it is so raises too many questions, many of which are irrelevant. A fairer statement would be that humanists are at home in Athens, not in Sparta, nor Jerusalem. Then Plato, a most glorious son of Athens, finds his affinity in Sparta. Has he gone over to the enemy and become the enemy? Not merely by taking up another point of view, and even if he aspires to remodel Athens on Sparta, he is not the enemy unless and until he conspires to do so. For Athenians have to abide the challenge of Sparta – or of Jerusalem. As Croce expressed it, as a liberal under the challenge of fascism:

A moral or political ideal that regards its contrary with total and sterile rejection is condemned by its incapacity to transcend the virtues and meet without damage the needs represented by the other ideal.

Yet it is illusion to think that there can be this total ideal, that there can be choice without renunciation, life without death. Croce himself is more realistically idealistic in a later context of his *History of Europe in the 19th Century* where he says:

And with regard to what is present and actual, it is necessary to examine, and in every case to re-examine, the ideals that today are accepted, or proposed, or tested, to see whether they have the power to dissolve or overcome, or correct our own ideal, and at the same time to change or modify it in consequence of the criticism through which it passes, and, in every case, to possess it again in firmer fashion.

The humanist needs the saint in order to become more

firmly his chosen self. The saint, exemplar of a rejected ideal, is not the enemy; but the Church, which is formed on this ideal, may be. The eighteenth-century humanists denounced 'kings' and 'priests' as the enemy, since they stood for oppression and obscurantism against the cause of emancipation and enlightenment with which the progress and happiness of mankind were bound up. Voltaire, however, the arch-enemy of the church in France (*écrasez l'infame*), did not attack the humble minister of the gospel, but the priest corrupted by political authority and power, the inhuman Theocracy by which France was ruled.

Some have argued that 'liberals' as opponents of oppressors and obscurantists should be and should be happiest in the communist camp with friends who are the sworn enemies of the master class and its lackeys. There is no logic in this because liberals do not accept the communist premise of a 'class enemy'. Here, again, Croce speaks for the liberals:

Ideals may well be theoretically divided into good and bad, into superior and inferior, but men – and the actual battle is one of men against men – cannot thus be divided and set off against one another, and each one of them contains within himself in varying degree the true and the false, the high and the low, spirit and matter. Each one, no matter how reactionary he may profess to be or may boast of being, can, in the concrete case, defend and further liberty, and no matter how liberal he may think himself, can go over to the other side.

The test is not the party label but the stand taken when the conflict comes. From the communist point of view the humanist is a mere liberal, incapable of steadfastly recognizing the enemy and incapable of implacably destroying him when the time is right: he is therefore himself doomed to destruction. Notoriously, the democratic socialist is the worst enemy of all, the class betrayer. Therefore the humanist can hardly think of the communist as a friend who is against all the hereditary enemies of the humanist, only more so. It is not as simple as that, although there are some humanists simple enough to believe that it is.

All the same, there is a real danger that the humanist as a

liberal, as tolerant, as interested in all things human, may be too unready to take sides and make a stand when the case requires it. Sartre for this reason indicts three generations of Frenchmen brought up in a liberal humanism of this kind. Bred in this tradition, they were unable to recognize in Nazism an enemy to be opposed by all means and at all costs, not merely a social phenomenon to be studied and understood. Therefore they betrayed civilization. On the other hand, M. N. Roy was a humanist of eighteenth-century temper who made precisely this recognition in circumstances in which he had to take sides and make his stand with the hereditary enemy (the British) against the Japanese fascists and against Gandhi and his own friends in his own party. This moral discrimination and the moral courage to stand by one's own insight and to desert one's friends when they confront the wrong enemy may be required of the humanist. Loyalty is not enough, if it means to be in a camp, to wear a label, to herd with the flock and know the whistle and the bark. The leader may be deadly wrong. Shaw was.

In all history there has hardly been a clearer case of all-black evil embodied in a party in power than the case of the Nazis. Yet the responsibility for Hitler's Germany lay mainly with the Allied victors in the First World War who disposed of supreme power to mould the conditions of post-war Europe. Their Europe produced Hitler's Germany. Neither they themselves nor the elements they recognized had any remedy for the intractable problems which reduced the German people to despair. Only the new untried men offered new remedies which promised to work. Even this is an over-simplification, but the truth is that real problems are insoluble because the steps that would have prevented them were not taken and later cannot be taken. Tragedy takes its fatal course, and it is only in the future that one may hope to do better because something has been learned. Thus even European civilization versus Nazidom – repeat, one of the clearest of all cases – was not innocence resisting guilt. But all our post-Freudian and post-Marxian psychology and sociology, all the sophistication needed to understand and interpret Nazism, to know what was going on, could not have justified non-resistance. There is a point of no-return.

The ultimate question of politics is, who shall kill whom? One political philosophy prescribes that one should always work to get into the position in which to force that ultimate issue with a calculated chance of disposing of the enemy and remaining master of the field. Another political philosophy sees the whole art of politics as the avoidance and the evasion of this ultimate issue. Conflicts are mitigated, institutionalized, policed, somehow reduced to a manageable level short of forcing that ultimate issue. The attempt is to live with conflicts safely, not to get rid of them definitively. In this philosophy, violence is not merely a further, and at some point necessary, step in politics, but rather the failure and breakdown of politics. This second philosophy is the humanist philosophy of politics, but, as Machiavelli recognized, history does not always allow the humanist to practise his ideals. To survive he may have to beat the enemy at his own game. But so far as he can determine the conditions himself he will strive to establish or to maintain the conditions of agreement and good faith which are the essentials of a liberal social order of free institutions. What Walter Bagehot called 'government by discussion', what is really government by negotiation and agreement, is the only tolerable way of conducting human affairs in the humanist view. When for any reason it is not possible, the object is to make it possible.

Ideally, then, the humanist is not afraid to take sides and he is not afraid to change sides. He is not afraid to make a stand and he is not afraid to give way. He is not afraid to wear a label nor to throw it away. His chronic discrimination, moderation, flexibility, relativism makes him an unreliable party man, an untrustworthy fighting comrade. He is using the party rather than serving the party. His loyalties inspire no confidence. Is this his true political character?

Yes and no. Seen from the outside, he may look like that, unreliable and unpredictable, not heart and soul with the cause. Yet if the consistent pattern of his conduct is discerned he is seen to be entirely reliable and predictable. For the clue to his conduct is a first and last loyalty to the humanist cause. Like Socrates he may be an uncomfortable comrade, but he will never be a dirty one.

The Humanist Cause

As a phrase 'the humanist cause' may sometimes serve a rhetorical purpose, but can it ever serve a moral purpose? To be loyal to the humanist cause in all one's allegiances and fights may be merely a presumptuous way of phrasing oneself out of any real commitment at all. How does it work?

How much easier and more comfortable to think that all Catholic mothers are bad mothers because you know they bring up their children to reverence and obey the priest and to believe a farrago of superstitious and wicked nonsense, than to identify the woman next door as a bad mother because she punishes her child in a way that frightens him so that he totally submits, equally afraid of her hostility and aggression against him and of his against her. In the first case you can indulge in verbal attack upon the Catholic Church and all its works, and join a society to that end. In the second case, what do you do?

Or you are a doctor who knows colleagues whose practices are unfair to their patients and tend to run down and discredit the National Health Service. Or you are on the shop floor and know what is going on which undermines the prestige and authority of the Union, or you know of practices which threaten the production and development of the firm. What do you do?

Wherever the humanist is he will never be far from cases of this kind. Wherever he is there will be the public-spirited line which will seem to others officious, priggish, uncalled for, and there will be the line of least resistance, the way of the world doing as others do. There *is* such a thing as officious, priggish, uncalled-for interference, just as there genuinely is moral courage and public spirit. To dodge the duty of the one by identifying it with the unpleasant superfluity of the other must always be tempting to the ordinary person who doesn't like officiousness. This is practically an abandonment of any pretence at moral conduct, however. For it was never enough to do oneself what is morally required; it was always necessary to require the same of others. Otherwise, morality makes victims instead of giving security, and the moral fabric of society is riddled. Long ago Cicero remarked that to be just meant not only to refrain from injustice but also to protect others from injustice. Innocence is not enough. Public spirit is also necessary. Therefore the 'enemy' may be the man next door or one's own brother, or anyone at all from time to time, if the moral realities, on which ultimately a human life for all depends, are to be consistently upheld.

Thus 'the actual battle is one of men against men', as Croce says. And the men to be fought [in the humanist cause] are bigots, sectarians, dogmatists, fanatics, hypocrites, whether Christians or humanists, and all those, however labelled, who seek for any purpose whatever to dupe, enslave, manipulate, brain-wash, or otherwise deprive human beings of their self-dependence and responsibility, all those particularly who victimize thus the young and inexperienced. The humanist cause, in the vastest and vaguest of phrases, is 'life and freedom', and on the enemy front are all those doctrines, institutions, practices and people hostile to life or freedom.

Dealing with the Enemy

Having identified the 'enemy', how does the humanist proceed against him? The rule for the humanist is, as stated before, to discern and to respect in the enemy the human being, the better and worse, the fund of possibilities, the responsible person. Therefore the first move is to try to get him to behave responsibly. That is, he has to be made fully aware of what he is doing in the light of its consequences. If nevertheless he persists, he may have to be opposed. What this may mean in practice belongs to the situation, but the intention of the opposition is to bring about dissuasion, to effect a change of mind. This may not be possible by reasoning, since behaviour is seldom wholly rational and sometimes wholly irrational, and quite often rational in the given context but not in an ideal context. The humanist may want to dissuade the Roman Catholic from wanting his own schools, but he is not likely to do this by enlarging on the evils of indoctrination and segregation, if the Catholic has reason to know or to think that if his child goes to a State school in a country more or less hostile to his faith steps will be taken in one way or other to deprive him of that faith. The situation is quite different if the Catholic has reason to know or to think that he lives in a society which scrupulously respects personal conviction and steadfastly upholds group independence. In that case it is reasonable to press the arguments against segregation on all the fronts of common life. This case brings out the point that on humanist assumptions it is not the holder of other opinions or convictions, the chooser of other values, the practitioner of a different way of life who is the enemy, but rather the one who wishes to impose these on others, who may be the humanist himself in the name of the 'open society'. When the 'enemy' is identified as the advocate of denominational schools, he is not to be fought by seeking to deprive him of them but rather by seeking to deprive him of the justification for wanting them. This may seem highly idealistic, but nothing less is very realistic – in rational terms. Of course the issue can always be settled, as it usually is, by political strength.

Whatever the quarrel, public or private, there is an invariable general rule: one should not humiliate the enemy. Whatever is done to humiliate him, by putting him in the wrong, by showing contempt and superiority, merely establishes a second independent and unnecessary ground of hostility, harder to remove than the first. How can one not put the enemy in the wrong? Only by making it abundantly clear that one is on a footing of moral equality in sharing the same liability to be wrong.

This 'invariable rule' can be taken as a kind of warning sign: 'Sinking Sands'. For the friends–enemies situation is not at all times as firm and safe as it feels. 'Depth psychology' has shown how treacherous this ground may be. We normally long to feel 'safe and right' with our friends, confronting enemies on whom we are fully justified in unleashing our destructive anger and aggression. In a more personal way, we may 'choose' enemies, not because they are hostile to us, but because they represent characteristics we unconsciously dislike in ourselves. Without going further into this territory, it can be said that the 'enemy' as an object to be humiliated, punished, destroyed and the 'friend' as an object of unconditional and uncritical loyalty are not likely to be rational enemies and friends, least of all when the enemy and friend are groups or classes, not single persons. The humanist is committed to trying to 'live with reality', to come to terms with his own ambivalence and his own guilt and failure, and with that of others. So that he cannot allow himself to resort to uncritical identification with the absolute right and good in any form, nor can he afford himself the luxury of a 'scapegoat', vowed to destruction as absolute evil. He lives and acts in a world of better and worse possibilities, and he chooses allies and faces opponents in the cause which he judges will promote the better possibilities in the actual situation. Among these allies he may make personal friends. As Epicurus said, the utilitarian basis of friendship may support friendship for its own sake. But loyalty to allies and loyalty to personal friends are not one and the same thing. Loyalty to personal friends is in principle the more permanent bond, but to make this the highest and prior loyalty, and the main principle of liberal humanism with Mr E. M. Forster, is to go too far in the direction of the absolute.

Dealing with an opponent in the company of one's friends, one is dealing usually with an institution, a party, an entrenched and organized 'interest'. Both sides engage in propaganda and in political action. Both sides are in the main appealing to the uncommitted, to public opinion. Each side defends itself against misrepresentations, against the enemy's attempts to prejudice public opinion, and against more legitimate attacks on the position held. The arguments are not only for or against the central positions but also for or against policies advocated on general grounds of truth or public interest. Catholics are, perhaps, against abortion on some grounds and against euthanasia on any ground, as a matter of principle, whereas humanists may argue for these policies on humanitarian grounds. Both sides appeal to public opinion beyond their own ranks. Sometimes the argument is not merely against opinions or policies but against established positions and privileges. But in all cases the issues are argued, and the arguments are tested not merely by appeal to the facts of experience as in science, but in the end by appeal to votes. The suffrage of the majority determines what shall be done, and belief and persuasion determine the suffrage of the majority.

Standards of controversy are the joint responsibility of the parties engaged. They are an important part of public morals. Mutual abuse and misrepresentation are forms of violence and cunning which help to destroy mutual respect and trust required for co-existence and cooperation in a society. Therefore the necessary conflicts of controversy should not involve unnecessary violation of the spirit and the rules of public debate. On platforms, in the air, in the press, in books, these debates are in almost continuous session, and all the time honourable standards are being upheld or are being ignored. There is no more obvious measure of the level of public morals. Good relations with the 'enemy' is the condition and test of healthy controversy, and usually means that the enemies are on fairly equal terms. Mud-slinging in politics – and all controversy is politics – provokes mud-slinging in retort, but it usually begins with the despondent side, to put heart into adherents in danger of deserting to join the destructive power of an overwhelming enemy. The brutal terms which make communist controversy so unpleasant express anything but the confidence in history which is their political faith.

Enemy Categories

The injunction to love the enemy is at a merely personal level, and resolves no general issue. If I offer the other cheek, I disarm my attacker by demonstrating that I am not personally hostile, but at the same time I may differ radically in ideas and ideals and may be implacably opposed to his policies. If I do hate him personally because his policies and deeds are evil and I and mine have suffered from them, and if I work on myself and succeed over a period in liberating myself from that hatred, however wronged I have been, my state of mind can hardly be expressed in gestures and tactics and may not be directed to the offender himself at all but rather disclose itself in new attitudes and purposes towards others.

Public, as distinct from personal, enemies may be usefully classified as opponents, defaulters and gangsters. Opponents and defaulters may be numbered among one's personal friends – and so may gangsters if one happens to be a gangster. Defaulters and gangsters are enemies of the public, but opponents are public enemies in a different sense. They are not enemies of the public and they are not necessarily personal enemies, but they are enemies on grounds which can be made a public issue.

Opponents are on opposite sides, but may not be enemies in a serious sense, as in a game they obviously are not. Opponents in business or in a law-suit or in politics represent rival interests, each striving to prevail. The conflict, as in a game, is carried on within the rules; and the ups and downs and ins and outs of business and politics are not so clear-cut and decisive as wins and losses in games or at law. War was once plausibly described as a further step in politics, although the 'balance of power' strategy was devised to prevent any such step; and in 'war-game' thinking the calculation of risks in diplomatic bluff is supposed to be on a more precise footing and includes the risk of escalation of a 'limited war' controlled by the new 'balance of terror'. The rules for this game are less certain, more hazardous than any other, and the stakes are far higher. Therefore here opponents in armed conflict or on the edge of conflict really are enemies, threatening each other's lives and total interests. Religious and ideological wars have been the most bitter and destructive, but ideological oppositions are not in themselves likely causes of war. Competition in ideas and ideals is not the same thing as competition in trade, but in both cases the competition may be beneficial.

There is a general interest in 'healthy' competition within a society and between societies, and here 'healthy' usually means competition regulated by rules, in which opponents are out to excel one another rather than to destroy one another.

'Defaulters' are all those who fail to live up to the level of current knowledge and morals through ignorance, indolence, or selfishness, those who deliberately exploit to their own advantage the efficiency and dependability of others and those who simply could not care less about the consequences of their commissions and omissions. All of us are more or less defaulters over the years, and all are injured by the defaults. Although the defaulter is the enemy of all, he is particularly the enemy of those who are trying to uphold or to raise the level of public morality, the enemy of the public spirited. This is an enemy not to be destroyed in any sense, but to be won over. Indeed, 'attack' is here an exercise in prevention.

Whereas we are all defaulters more or less, gangsters are organized against society. Every developed society harbours predators who organize an underworld. A densely populated and industrialized and affluent society offers greater scope and therefore greater temptation to criminal brains and nerves. There are polytechnic resources to make use of and glittering prizes to seize. The criminal display may corrupt a society by compelling the admiration of a public prone to respond because continually entertained by crime on the screen. The gangs keep hitting the headlines, and the public does not feel the blows. Occasionally, the sensational coup thrills rather than appals a whole nation, and the savage reprisal of the authorities on those who are caught does nothing to redress the balance. If police are shot dead, the situation is dramatically reversed and popular sympathies are swung to the other side. But this is precisely audience-response not citizenship. Then there is the 'mafia' type organization which penetrates public life and is interwoven with normal society which it corrupts by bribery and intimidation; its voice is heeded but not heard; it rules and is not accountable, but ruthlessly settles accounts. The underworld may extend its tentacles everywhere and turn society upside down. Subversion of a society by criminal gangs can be thorough and persistent, resulting in a chronic malaise. Subversion by a political gang is likely to be swifter and more open and decisive. Nazism is the spectacular and special case, but it was a fellow conspirator with Fascism. Indeed, the police-State anywhere may fairly be said to be gangster-rule. It may not be 'criminal' because the law is perverted to sanction it, but it is not what is meant by 'the rule of law'.

This classification of enemies into the categories of personal enemies, opponents, defaulters, and gangsters is useful for two main reasons: mere opponents are often treated as personal enemies or even as enemies of mankind; the real enemies of mankind are insufficiently recognized and inadequately treated. Awareness of realities and a sense of proportion are particularly needed on these dangerous fronts, and are conspicuously lacking.

Old and New Enemies of the Humanists

To return from this discursive ramble to the hereditary enemies of the humanist, kings and priests. There are republican zealots and anti-clerical fanatics self-employed on these old enemies still, but that is not for want of more serious work to do.

The 'enemy' are those who attack the humanists and those whom the humanists attack, or should attack. Do these include the churches? Certainly humanists attack and want to do away with institutional privilege and to bring about the conditions of a truly open society in which all faiths are fully disestablished and freely respected. Churches which resist this and defend established privilege are to that extent the enemy. Christian spokesmen who misrepresent or denounce humanism make themselves the enemy. But this is the bad behaviour of 'opponents' who are 'defaulting'. They are entitled to oppose humanism with due fairness and respect, as humanists are entitled either to argue against Christianity or merely to differ from Christian fellow citizens. It is a good thing when Christians happen to number humanists amongst their personal friends, and vice versa. It is a good thing also when 'dialogue' is going on between Christians and humanists, because this keeps public contact between human beings who differ profoundly in their ultimate convictions, helps to rub out old stereotypes and to discard common misrepresentations, and, above all, defines more closely the areas of public co-operation and the areas of public contention. Christians who accept the 'open mind' and the 'open society' as major ideals, and who are ready to tackle realistically the common problems and tasks of a modern society, are surely better friends of the humanist than those who are fiddling sour old tunes regardless of what is really happening in Rome, or anywhere else. The seed of humanism is latent in the cultural tradition which the churches now share, and may spring up and flourish within the churches, bearing its characteristic fruits.

The Christian preacher who insists that without God man has no reason to live responsibly, the Christian teacher of biology who tacks on to evolutionary theory in the same tone of voice as an extra truth about man the doctrine he believes in, the marriage counsellor who treats a marriage that is not Christian as though it were or ought to be Christian: these are probably everyday occurrences, and there may be far worse examples of the same kind. Those who commit these destructive acts, for that is what they are, although they may do so in simple good faith, are in the category of defaulters. They fall short of what is right and required in our society, and reasonably to be expected. As defaulters, they are enemies of society, not merely of humanists but also of responsible Christians.

The 'little' enemy is the ubiquitous defaulter, in ourselves not least. But 'little' in the aggregate could amount to biggest of all. A high standard of scrupulous public-spirited morality is as necessary to society as public hygiene. 'The spiritual foundations of public opinion have to be watched with the same eternal vigilance with which we look after the physical foundations of our national defences.' *

* A humanist friend from abroad who in the chaos of his country during the war was possessed by a devastating passion of hatred for the persons responsible for the vilest evils he suffered and saw, and who

The 'big' enemy is the gangster, and he lurks in several shapes and is tough and determined. The underworld or shadow society of organized criminal gangs is the type of the 'big' enemy. A society which is fascinated by crime and finds its depiction a staple form of entertainment is not in a good state of mind to cope successfully with the reality of organized crime. This is one of the test questions for civilized societies. No less spectacular and searching is the race question. The racialist is the ugliest and most reckless gangster of all, for he forces the ultimate political question, who shall kill whom? in the most provocative and violent form. There is nothing more detestable, dangerous and contagious abroad in the world. Whether racialism is consolidated in the government and policy of a State or exists sporadically in segregation or discrimination, it is an evil to be fought as fire is fought.

The dissolution of colonial empires and the institution of

---

painfully delivered himself from this obsession, has sent me a MS 'Quixote and Zorba', a dialogue of two friends. I extract this passage from one of the speeches, as a comment on the 'little' enemies, the defaulters: 'But this "impotent hatred" as you call it is not only directed towards official monsters, as Verwoerd, Hitler, Churchill, Stalin, who make me despise my race. I would say that I hate even more the lesser bandits, liars, hypocrites, sharks, foxes, serpents, peacocks, whom I meet in everyday life or whose deeds I hear about at any moment. This hatred is even more lasting, or it repeats itself frequently. And it is hatred, because I do want their annihilation. I manage to convert this hatred into scorn, but there is not much difference between hatred and scorn. Those who easily could diminish some suffering of the other as it lies in their power, yet do not do it because of their nasty buttock-ethics. We are the same monsters in war and in peace. That is what is *puant* and nauseating in the human race. You must hate *that* if you feel a little bit different from them. And I cannot help it, tho I might be wrong, that I do feel a little bit different from them. The so-called little scandal of our race is even more repugnant than the free sabbath of cruelty in wars and revolutions. I feel that such a hatred makes me stronger and I don't want to give it up for any humanism. I don't want to struggle against it. I don't want to convert myself into a lamb. Nor do I wish to listen to any sermon of tolerance in face of them. Nausea is the answer, not tolerance. A revolt, not a toleration.'

the United Nations have not wiped out the imperialist mentality. Whether or not the policies and acts of a particular power are imperialistic may be a question, but the liability to use power to establish political dominion is not a question, and those powers who do it are gangsters.

Finally, highly organized advanced industrial societies are likely to throw up a new type of gangster who may be the deadliest of all. Worse than the old theocracies may be the new technocracies. The technical expert and the efficient administrative official are first-class valuable public servants, but as technocrats and bureaucrats who hog the decisions and manipulate men for the creation of some Brave New World, they would be the ultimate enemy. That particular essay in dehumanization for power is the last word in man's inhumanity to man.

If these defaulters and gangsters are the real enemies of the humanists, their friends and allies are all those who rally against these enemies. If many of these happen to be Christians, who will be surprised? And who will mind?

9

STRATEGY AND TACTICS

> One awful thing that the Book of the Past makes plain is
> that with our animal heritage we are singularly oblivious
> to the large concerns of life. We are keenly sensitive to
> little discomforts, minor irritations, wounded vanity, and
> various danger signals, but our comprehension is in-
> herently vague and listless when it comes to . . . establish-
> ing anything like a fair perspective in life's problems
> and possibilities.
>
> *James Harvey Robinson*

A Theory of Progress

A HUMANIST movement is rather like a political party of the
left. There are the radicals who think only of a rational reconstruction of society. There are the near-anarchists who are
uneasy about any form of social organization. There are the
realists who start with things as they historically are and pose
some modest measure of improvement to work for, and who
are ready to do a lot to gain a little. Radicals, anarchists and
realists do not make easy team-fellows, yet each has a necessary part of the humanist in him. The strategy of human advance finds room for them all. Tactics usually require the
dominance of one.

Of course a humanist movement is not at all a political
party. But it does stand for, and is pledged to work for, a particular view of human advancement. Therefore it is immersed
in politics, for always and everywhere the conditions of human
living are rough-hewn by political power and political
decisions. To stand aside from politics is to abandon the
world. Humanism is a concern to understand and to change
the world so that human life is more valuable to more people.
In this respect it is nearer to communism in type than to the
world religions. However, it remains decisively different from
both in the theory of human advancement and of the relations
between the social and the personal. If, for the sake of argu-

ment, the goals of Christianity, communism and humanism could be equally described as a community of free and equal persons, both the reality to be achieved and the means proposed for achieving it would be remarkably distinct, and distinctive, in each case. Therefore a description of humanism should include the humanist view of human advancement.

The kind of world the humanist wants to be able to live in has already been described in terms of the open mind and the open society. It is a world in which people can and do learn purposefully and continuously from experience (the open mind), and in which society is so organized by agreement that individuals and groups are allowed and enabled by the cooperation to live lives of their own, rich in choices (the open society). This excludes ultimate interpretations, values and ends from social theory, and locates them solely within the provinces of personal and group life in the society. Equal room is left for faith in Providence and for the humanist assumption that there is no purposive order at all in nature or history.

Essentially, this view sees the problem of human advancement as the advancement of learning (in Bacon's phrase); this learning is not only scientific advancement but also advancement in other forms of learning, a cumulative process of learning methodically from experience in every way. This is a rational view of human progress, and technically it is entirely feasible. Politics could be (and partly is) a systematic way of learning from collective experience what people want and how to get it. The problem is that human behaviour is far from rational, that men are short-sighted and their own worst enemies. A pessimistic reading of history easily gathers plenty of evidence from the recorded behaviour of men down the ages to justify distrust of any view of human progress that simply says: 'We know how to solve our problems. We can improve conditions for all.' Faith in man is not less hard to justify than faith in God. A religious view of the world has always been bound up with a sense of the fatality of things and the futility of unaided human effort. Apart even from their own selfishness and destructiveness, men get involved in events which they have not willed and cannot control. Many serious problems reach a stage when they are insoluble, although it may be apparent how they might have been prevented. To say that human existence is tragic is to anticipate too much, but to pretend that mankind today is not the survivor of innumerable tragedies is sheer perversity or an ignorance that is more depressing than history itself. The tragedies, greater and less, which mankind have survived were hardly ever inevitable (although they probably became so beyond a point of no-return) and hardly ever creative in any sense at all. The question is whether we can reasonably hope to learn to prevent them or hope only to go on surviving them. On some religious assumptions men can never do better without the aid of a power beyond their own. But history hardly warrants the hope that faith will save *the world* – to appeal to a practical test. On humanist assumptions, we can do better only by dealing effectively with ourselves.

If human advancement comes by learning from experience how to prevent problems by maintaining a creative initiative and how to solve them in due time before they become insoluble, then the task is to make this learning more likely and more reliable. The strategy and tactics of human advance lie in creating and maintaining the conditions of the advancement of learning in this total sense. What follows is intended to indicate the role of a humanist movement in helping to shape what is to come.

Humanism in Politics

Humanists in the context of a tradition-bound religion-dominated society have naturally leaned to the political parties that stood for change, but there is no reason why a humanist should not be a good tory, and some at least are. The proper question is not whether humanism inclines to the left, nor how much it does so, but what kind of political action is appropriate to the kind of movement which humanism is.

The focus of politics is in legislation and the established public policy which it represents and which governs its administration. Surrounding the laws and established policies is public opinion, supporting them or opposing them. Politics express in action formed bodies of public opinion, or seek to influence opinion. The battle is for and against laws and public policies all of which forbid or require or allow certain things to be done, and thus determine the framework of human living in the society. In the chapter 'The Open Society' the distinction was made between laws which are 'rules of the road' regulating private conduct and laws which are 'rules of the game' because they constitute and set going a common social institution or purpose. The greater part of modern legislation is social planning of this latter kind.

However elaborate and far-reaching these national plans may be, they do not of themselves realize the hopes they bear. They may be the target of long endeavour, but they remain only the beginning of possible achievement. What actually happens in the classrooms does more for the education of the nation before and after 1944 than the Education Act. The educational philosophy embodied in the Act of that year was generous and far-sighted, but in practice the letter killed the spirit, and the experience of that failure has turned public policy to the trial of 'comprehension'. Administrative devices may apologize for personal failures of one kind or another, but they never compensate. Legislation like revolution is always a goal of hopes, and often a graveyard. Politics are about legislation and have the limits of legislation. At the same time they have the enormous importance in human affairs which belongs to the power to create and to obstruct opportunity, to decide between better and worse possibilities. Itself 'the art of the possible', the art of politics is not merely limited by what can be done, it also settles what can be done. The Act of 1944 was limited in the attempt to establish a public system of education by the claims of the churches, but it also settled the procedures which should govern religion in the county schools and the conditions on which church schools should be entitled to aid from public funds. Much more important, the Act steered the nation towards 'comprehension' whether or not the comprehensive school is the answer.

Always to bear equally in mind the importance and the limits of political activity is a difficulty perhaps easier for a humanist movement than for the individual member. It is a maxim for headquarters at congresses and at all times. A more practical difficulty at the heart of politics is control of the executive. Any society must have acknowledged authorities with the power to take decisions and to enforce them, that is to say a government. This power is always at the same time the security of and a danger to the interests affected, that is to say the governed. Attempts to limit without unduly hampering the power of government, to identify the interests of the governors with those of the governed, to make them responsible to and replaceable by the governed, make some of the most interesting and instructive pages of history. The high hopes of constitutional devices and democratic slogans ('the sovereignty of the people') have not been entirely realized, although political democracy, that is to say the possibility of politics, has been enjoyed in some places to an extent that makes it as strong and primary a value to society as health is to the person. Even in the most successful democracy the difficulty of keeping the executive responsible does and must remain. Like social legislation, constitutional devices do not work automatically. They provide only opportunities for control. The onus is on people, and not only the official Opposition, although in the Opposition are concentrated the interest, the skill, the experience, the time, the energy, the proximity, the facilities, the duty which are likely to make the most effective body for the surveillance of the executive in the way designed to keep it continuously responsible and sensitive to public opinion. But inspectors of inspectors are required even when there are none. The substance of the question is older than Juvenal: *Quis custodiet ipsos custodies?*

There is always the press, and it is always important. But all the institutions and procedures for the purpose do not guarantee the responsibility of the government in a democracy. The responsibility for responsibility belongs to the citizens themselves, and cannot be delegated. The citizen may feel mocked by his democratic responsibilities, and slide into indifference in sheer helplessness. Correspondents to the newspapers frequently express this despair. For example:

> Thus it is possible to turn the taxation system under which industry and commerce operate inside out in a matter of months without consulting any of the interests affected, but nothing can be done about eyesores such as Piccadilly Circus, or the desecration of Oxford by traffic, or the derelict site opposite the Victoria and Albert Museum in Kensington owing to sheer administrative anarchy.*

This particular groan may or may not be reasonable, except as a sign of pain, but the points to be made are: decisions have to be made, and sometimes have to be delayed; whatever happens, some interests will be injured or angered; governments are always fallible, may be incompetent or perverse in their decisions and indecisions, and need the support and criticism of all citizens at all times. Vital decisions with far-reaching consequences may be taken behind closed doors on the basis of only expert advice and information and with a view to administrative convenience. This danger of rule by a faceless technocratic *élite* is more present and real in a parliamentary democracy than rule by a corrupt secret police. But 'closed circles' of uncontrolled power, venal or not, can exist at all levels of public life, in cultural, social and industrial as well as political institutions, and they can exist and operate in every kind of society, even under a formal dictatorship (for example, Yugoslavia) and even in a political democracy.

All citizens are responsible to one another for the responsibility of their rulers at all levels of authorized decision-making. The competent authorities have to be *enabled* and *required* to be responsible. They have to be enabled to be responsible 1. by being kept informed of the interests affected by the decisions they take and 2. by being able to rely on the support of the interests affected, so that they can take effective decisions. They have to be required to be responsible by being in fact answerable, subject to recall, and by being judged by

* *The Times*, Letters to the Editor, 9 August 1966.

their performance as authorities required and enabled to act responsibly by those to whom they are responsible. Thus the citizens are themselves fully responsible for the responsible behaviour of their rulers. Without responsible and disciplined citizens, democratic institutions cannot constitute democracy. In this sense people get only the rulers they deserve. Over-aggressive pressure groups, anarchistic individualists, apathetic people, make responsible government impossible. Responsible representative government is an active partnership. The conflicts are there, and may be serious, but they are institutionalized and disciplined; they are conducted, controlled and resolved by responsible politics.

The fruits of an open society are a secure and rich private life for individuals and groups, and they are the fruits of close and loyal collaboration in the interdependence which supports this independence. This collaboration depends on broad agreements continually revised or renewed, especially necessary and difficult in a densely populated and highly organized and complicated industrial society. These agreements can hardly be reached nor maintained unless certain conditions prevail. Majority rule is generally recognized as no more than an expedient device for settling whose will shall prevail. And it is also recognized that the device is worthless unless minorities are treated considerately and their right to try to turn themselves into a majority is strictly respected, for otherwise they would be virtually excluded from the society and would become enemy outlaws. If sectional interests are invited to make themselves victims in the name of the public interest, anarchy will supervene. Equitable conditions, social justice, must be seen to be politically attainable if the broad agreements required to manage the economy are to be attainable and maintainable. Public spirit is required, but is not to be expected except as the mutual protection of enjoyed interests. Individualism properly belongs to the superstructure of independence supported by interdependence, but it cannot be kept to its proper place if its legitimate wants and claims are ignored or overridden in the other place.

These considerations belong to the ethos and practice of

democracy and affect the public responsibility of all private citizens. They intimately concern the humanist movement because its hopes and aims are bound up with the development of an open society and the advancement of mankind, understood as the advancement of learning. How can a humanist movement help its members to become politically effective, and by the help of its members itself be politically effective? Particularly to be borne in mind is the responsibility which all citizens share for the responsibility of their rulers and the responsibility which they all share for each other's public behaviour. Responsibility is closely shared and ultimately indivisible through this domain of the public conduct of public affairs, and this recognition informs what follows about the agents, methods and subjects of political action in a humanist movement.

A humanist movement can act directly in a political way in its own name, or indirectly through its members, its own local or special groups, the international organization to which it belongs, lobbies it may set up or special associations it may support. A further word about some of these.

Humanist movements have always encouraged their members to play an active part of their own in public life in one way or another. They have been nurseries of talent for and interest in public affairs. Particularly in the years of reform, when there seemed all to do for the achievement of social justice, public service in politics was the way of action marked out for those inspired by humanist ideals. One of the Ethical Societies turned itself into a branch of the Independent Labour Party and adopted and returned Keir Hardie. So complete an identification with party politics, however, is out of character. The local group or the total movement as mother, as nursery, as home provides the formative influence, the moral anchorage, the point of return for the common humanity of men and women who decide for themselves, guided by their own reading of experience and events and their own choice of possibilities. With the reduction of party differences this social function becomes more practicable, bringing and holding together in the fellowship of a common inspiration men and women of different political persuasions and others whose political activity cuts across party lines. In such a milieu the politically minded and the socially minded are in touch with one another in the most sympathetic way. This may be of great consequence.

A humanist movement is a general movement for a universal end, not a specialized association for a specific object. This is at once its difficulty and its justification in an age of intense specialization. The difficulty is of being recognized to stand for any purpose at all, and the danger of being diffuse. The justification is that man as a whole person and humanity as a single interest need all the more to be represented and expressed. Such a movement loses its *raison d'être* if it allows itself to become preoccupied with certain issues and to drift into becoming a pressure-group devoted to these issues. If there are special associations already for these objects, they will have the expertise and should be aided with personnel or otherwise as and when needed. Where there is no special association, a humanist movement may be called to set one up, or some of its members may together take this initiative. The movement can and should work with and through such agencies, and may maintain close liaison with some of them, but these are the resources to which it contributes and on which it relies and draws, as opportunity serves or priority requires, in the prosecution of its own comprehensive purposes.

The International Humanist and Ethical Union is a nongovernmental organization on the register of the United Nations and with UNESCO. This involves obligations which are onerous in so far as they are taken seriously. The temptation for NGOs is to make only a nominal response to what is required of them or open to them. The temptation for the governments politically active at the UN (if not their concerted policy) is to cut out the NGOs so that they don't have to be taken into account. Here is a theatre of international politics in which what goes on has a bearing on the future of mankind if international institutions and policies are going to develop into the rudiments of a world order. That NGOs should hold on to their part and seek to enlarge its scope in these still early days may be of first-class importance. It means faithfulness and effectiveness in rather unrewarding work. But the stake is tomorrow.

Local humanist groups are addressed primarily, though not exclusively (for example, Amnesty undertakings), to their neighbourhood. They can find out what is going on politically and socially, and decide what most requires to be done from a humanist point of view. They can help the national organization to carry out investigations or concerted action. They can be helped by the national organization to carry out their own initiatives. They are the hands and feet of the movement. But locally they have relations with and loyalties to other bodies with whom they are responsible for the conditions of the place.

By what extra-parliamentary methods is political activity carried on? These are familiar enough, and may be divided into direct and indirect. Indirect would be such activities as forums, conferences, research, publications in the press and otherwise. Direct would be lobbying, demonstrations, resolutions, campaigns. Indirect methods are concerned to inform and form public opinion; direct methods also aim at public opinion, but nearer the point and place of policy decisions. A humanist movement can and should help its members to make up their minds on questions of the day by arranging conferences, circulating material for study, carrying out research, organizing discussion. Of course this is not to be done on every question of the day, nor in the manner of a class on current affairs, but such action can be taken on questions of selected concern; and it is a necessary preliminary to any concerted direct action that might be taken.

Groups of humanists took part in the Campaign for Nuclear Disarmament as declared humanists, but the Campaign was not endorsed officially by the organized movement. Organized humanists do keep members who are prepared to be politically active alerted and informed on matters of humanist interest, so that they write to the press or other organs of opinion in a timely and relevant way, or to their MPs or Ministers. Of course motions on current affairs are always forthcoming at general meetings, especially if there is some burning issue in the news. These may be voted with acclaim or with reluctance, perhaps with some lame or laming amendments. In any case the resolution is likely to be an example of irresponsible non-action. Pronouncements on public affairs by their organizations are passionately desired by some members of churches, and equally by members of a humanist movement. There is a public for such leads, and they may be influential. The likelihood of their really being influential depends on their competence and authority. An intervention so cogent and timely that it rallies public opinion to force a government to explain and justify its policy does not happen every day nor by good luck. To play this part effectively occasionally requires continuous application by students of affairs who include some actively engaged in public affairs at a responsible level. A pronouncement which puts forward a ready-made policy and implicitly tells the government what to do will be and must be ignored. A pronouncement can hardly be ignored if it is obviously well-informed and reasonably argued and asks for explanations or raises questions or draws attention to considerations which seem to have been overlooked or makes certain representations or justifies objections or registers a plain protest. Statements of this kind have a good chance of publicity and do help to keep a government or a Minister responsible. This is one way in which the general responsibility for responsibility in public affairs can be carried out. It seems one of the easiest, but if a decent standard of competence and effectiveness is to be attained it is most exacting.

Finally, what are the subjects on which humanists as humanists are concerned with political action? Any definite answer would belie the character of a humanist movement by making it a specialized association. There is hardly anything in the whole range of human affairs which is not of humanist interest. All the same, there are present priorities and there are special concerns. Humanity itself is under threat from international insecurity, population increase and unequal economic development. The humanist movement does not have specific answers of its own to these major global problems, but it is concerned to keep them on the agenda, to keep up the attack, to make contributions. If all organized bodies of opinion and effort would do just this, the problems would be reduced and managed. On domestic fronts there is the removal or modification of unnecessarily oppressive laws, most of which come down from a time when society had an accepted religious basis. Enlightenment and Emancipation, translated into contemporary international terms as Education and Human Rights, are still the dominant interests, and political action in these spheres is only one phase of the operation.

Above all, not the least part of this work of enlightenment and emancipation is education in politics, the continuous attempt to keep people alert, informed, active, so that the competent authorities of all kinds are made responsible because kept responsive. This educative task is particularly the political function of a humanist movement, helping and enabling people to carry and to discharge their share of responsibility for responsibility, rather than trying to do it for them.

Public Morality

Three purposes prompt humanist political interventions to make sure that public policy decisions are rationally and responsibly taken. 1. To seek disclosure of the information on which a decision is to be or has been taken; and to press for research if the information is unreliable or inadequate. 2. To discover the extent of consultation of interests affected and of agreement obtained. 3. To resist or protest against laws or public policies which are concerned with interests that properly belong to the sector of private life and personal choice.

Politics are frivolous unless taken in connexion with something someone is wanting or trying to do or to get. The resort to politics is forced when the existing state of affairs proves unsatisfactory. The attempt to work within existing laws and policies comes first – and last. What in general are humanists doing or wanting to see done that gives them this political point of reference? The social services (taken in the broadest sense to include education and housing and town-planning) are a central humanist interest because they are engaged in improving the conditions of life for all. Whether professionally engaged in any of them or not, humanists are particularly interested in the way in which these services are working and working out. As members of the public they can inquire and visit. They can do voluntary service, and gain first-hand information. Particularly, a local humanist group can undertake this investigation-of-by-participation-in the social services. This can be done by the group on its own or by forming local committees or by participation in the work of existing local groups, such as CASE, concerned with the advancement of State education.

The social services may be improved in three ways by such voluntary participation: 1. a direct stimulation of performance; 2. an improvement of conditions brought about by rousing interest and forming local opinion; 3. a contribution to the experience of better and worse possibilities under existing legislation in the light of which revisions can take place in due course with some certainty of advance.

Political intervention and social participation for these purposes, together with the public spirit exemplified in observing all the common rules and requiring others to do so, constitute a public morality that upholds the conditions of rationality and responsibility in public affairs. On these conditions a steady advancement of social learning from experience is possible. Of course such a public morality is not a monopoly of humanists and is not specifically humanist, or it would not be public morality. Plenty of people who abhor the assumptions of humanists are law-abiding citizens who vote duly in elections and write as occasion requires to their MPs or the press, are active members of CASE or some other local group of vigilant citizens, and never throw down litter themselves nor allow others to do so without a remonstrance. Such public morality may be convenient to the authorities, but will it advance mankind towards utopia? Public morality on these or any other lines may be formal and feeble or personal and vigorous, conformist or critical, and the difference makes all the difference.

Public morality which upholds the conditions of rationality and responsibility in public affairs is only regulative. The positive content of political action, the professional skills and standards of social service, the spontaneity of public spirit have other sources. But these creative influences are liable to be wasted or even destructive without the regulation of public morality. For humanists, public morality like society itself is mainly a means to personal ends. But means when they work well are valuable and enjoyable in themselves and a prompt and active public morality adds its own lustre to the light of personal existence.

Public Education

Education has always been the cardinal activity and the main hope of a humanist movement. For enlightenment is education and emancipation requires it. The self-dependent man who is not the dupe nor the tool of others and is master of his own resources is an educated man whether or not he has had the advantages of formal education. If he has won this independence, the sense in which he will also be cooperative depends more on the terms offered him by society than on education. For education of whatever kind takes place in a particular society and for that society – or possibly against it.

Education in an advanced society has always had three main phases or aspects: 1. acquisition of the basic knowledge and skills required by the society; 2. induction into the manners and customs, virtues and values, of the society; 3. development of the learner's own aptitudes and interests. These technical, moral and personal aspects of education are interdependent and concurrent; and they are equally important from the point of view of public policy, although they may not always be equally important in the proper education of a given child. Short-sighted views of parents and employers, sometimes of teachers, and perhaps of governments, may emphasize the first aspect to the neglect of the others. Humanists should stand for the proper balance, and for a high proportion of the national resources to be devoted to education in all its phases, as the most valuable social investment.

Technical education, that is, all the academic studies, the sciences and practical arts and the humanities and fine arts, is best able to take care of itself. There is a strong tradition to support it, and its practical fruits are highly appreciated and greatly needed by society. What does not take care of itself, however, is academic freedom. The freedom to appoint teachers, to develop new subjects and courses and lines of research, to organize the balance of teaching and research, has to be reconciled with the dependence of higher education on public funds and the need for public control over scientific manpower and research priorities. Also the problem of reconciling specialization with general education has not been solved, and the bifurcation of 'the two cultures' is here.

Moral education begins with birth. It can be thought of as induction into the family, into the school, into the peer group, and thus through special communities into the general society. Everything depends on the character and conduct of these special communities and of the society to which they belong. There is nothing called 'moral education' which can do better than they do. Moral education is primarily social experience. The experience of being dependably cared for and firmly restrained, of being morally weaned and enabled to become competent and self-dependent and cooperative should be the first phase of moral education, but induction into the family is not always like that. The nursery school can be very important where the home is inadequate. If a family does not have the knowledge, skill and will to bring up children in the early formative years, that is a 'problem family' for society whether or not listed as such. It is a matter of degree, and more can always be done to prepare those concerned for responsible parenthood.

At school, moral education should be the experience of being an equal member of a happy community engaged in thriving activities aimed at excellence, an experience of approvals and disapprovals and the discussion of them, an experience of rule-making and of the maintenance and enforcement of rules and the criticism of them. Beyond that, it is experience of the world outside by school groups who go out to find out and then discuss and tackle problems they identify. Moral education is the individual experience of boys and girls in their lives and contacts brought out in the classroom and examined and compared. This education in reflection and criticism and discrimination is the bridge between social education as induction into communities as they are and the moral experience of good communities (say, at school) or the moral vision of better possibilities. Experience of the bad and of the good, reflection on them and discussion of them, leading to an acceptance of responsibility for them: this is the age-old course of moral education about which we know more and do less than we think.

The educational community concentrated on its educational tasks and ideals draws its members from different milieux with different ideas and ideals of life – unless it is a denominational school. The common basis of their life together is in the rules and institutions of the school and its tasks and achievements. Differences in views and ways of life are accepted and respected. They reflect the situation outside, and social education together already establishes the cardinal distinction between public and private realms which is the basis of the open society. Moral education in a denominational school is induction into a homogeneous community, which is poor moral preparation for life in an open society and coexistence in a world order. Because without the appropriate social experience, moral education is a dubious name for pious hopes.

The education of the person for himself is not the least important aspect of education, even for society. A choice of curriculum comes before a choice of life. The child needs to have open to him a choice of activities and subjects by which he will be stimulated and developed. Of course 'child-centredness' is established doctrine in pedagogy, but the principle is far-reaching. Education for an open mind as well as an open society, for a life of one's own as well as for life in common, is not in the text-books. To learn to discern alternatives, to make comparisons, to form standards, to decide and to choose, to grasp the practical interdependence of idea and action and of the ideal and the actual, to learn to create and to manage an experience of one's own, even to learn how to think and how to argue and how to listen: all this belongs to the education of the person for himself, but one is lucky to have it in any institution of learning. Techniques of this kind enable one to convert the arts and sciences to one's own use. Unless culture is for the sake of life, education is of no avail. All citizens should come from their formal education with the will and the method to live lives of their own to some purpose.

The Humanist Role

Think of all that is going on to improve the human lot for more people by means of the U N and its special Agencies, the N G Os, government aid programmes, special commissions, and at home through the range of social services including education. The steady work, unnoticed on many fronts, must one day result in cumulative advance which will surprise the historian. All that is needed, all that can be done, is to put steadily more effort into what is being done now, and, funding in training what is learned from experience, raise continually the standard of skill and effectiveness. Here, the realistic humanist may think, is scope enough for the utmost human endeavour. The radical humanist is shocked by such complacency. He speaks of crisis and extreme urgency, and calls for leadership and new initiatives and concerted plans, a real strategy of human advance, a rallying of forces in an all-out effort to halt drift, avert disaster and put man in control of his destiny. Both types of thinking are pointless, however, if they are unrelated to the thinking of those who actually wield power and take the decisions.

The strategic thinking which has first to be reckoned with is the thinking of those in control of the USA as leader of 'the free world' and of those in control of the USSR as the formerly unchallenged leader of communist States and parties. The more problematical thinking of the rulers of China tomorrow has also to be taken into account. The 'peaceful coexistence of different social systems' is the main guideline of present Soviet foreign policy. Containment of communist expansion is the main guideline of present US foreign policy. These are not antithetical principles, and with the massive power wielded by both parties a balance of power form of world order has been established. American strategists probably hope to stabilize this order by reinforcing the trends towards forms of regionalism that will contain and reduce excessive nationalism, by building bridges across the regional frontiers, and by halting the spread of nuclear weapons, leading to some arms reduction and control. This, in the main, is not an unlikely sketch of the hopeful shape of things to come for world order and world development. This better possibility of course does not rule out worse possibilities. They appear as threatened realities in Cuba and Vietnam. Blunders have made history and are still making it.

What has all this to do with humanism? Well, humanism as an organized movement is situated in the 'free world' camp. Humanist ideals and aspirations are vested in the open mind and the open society, and depend on conditions possible at present mainly in the free world. This does not mean that humanists are tied to the tail of American foreign policy. It does mean that the prospect for realizing humanist ideals is bound up with the prudent and skilful management of a world policy which includes peaceful coexistence, the containment of communism, the development of regionalism, arms reduction and control. These are principles of world order, not of nationalism, and represent a common interest. It is a policy to which both the USSR and the USA have contributed and may be expected to contribute, although they see it in very different ways and with contrary hopes and expectations. Whatever influence humanists can have personally and by means of their organized movements national and international should be exerted on public opinion and on governments to press on to current objectives that promise to reinforce world order, with these guidelines in mind.

At home a humanist movement is a flexible instrument for education in politics, in social service, in public spirit, that is for mutual education in rationality and responsibility in all public affairs, and for help in practice. Humanists have a special interest in promoting these conditions of social rationality and responsibility but they are not alone. All those are with them who hate to see society enfeebled by 'defaulters' or ruined by 'gangsters', all 'lovers of man's perfection', all who find social health and sanity in freedom and equality properly regulated. Modern humanists are heirs of the *philosophes*, and the social rationality and responsibility indicated in this chapter follow on the enlightenment and emancipation which they proclaimed and for which they worked.

Humanism is education not only in means but also in ends, not only in social conditions but also in personal living. Here humanism is of use only to its own sons. And here spontaneity is the rule, and achievement the only guide. But company and encouragement are needed, and can be provided. Religion provided a First Cause which guaranteed the rationality of secondary causes, a Final Purpose to warrant that there is purpose which can and shall be fulfilled, and an eternal world to save from mockery the values of this world. Without guarantors, humanism has to sustain confidence and hope. The humanist has to walk by sight, but he is often in the dark, liable to be lost, and sometimes in a desert. If all can be lost, fears are not groundless, if dangers and difficulties loom large despair is near, if the enemy is found within, and entrenched, in whom can there be confidence? Only because final values have been tasted and tested is a secular civilization possible. Everything is not to be postponed to bless a happier generation, for that is the bitterest mockery of all. To make more abundant and more secure and more developed what is already in our hands and in our hearts is the meaning and measure of the task, the source of our confidence, the guide of our hopes. The responsibility of the humanist is response before it is answerability. He has responded and tasted, and therefore he takes on responsibility and makes exertions, for himself and for others.

QUESTIONS AND OBJECTIONS

Man is an intellectual animal, and therefore an everlasting contradiction to himself.
William Hazlitt

If one does not hope, one will not find the unhoped-for, since there is no trail leading to it and no path.
Heraclitus

ALL the usual questions and objections which are raised in the minds of many people by the ideas they have of what humanism is can already be answered out of the previous chapters. In this last chapter explicit answers to some of them are offered. This may serve as a summary of a good deal of what has gone before.

1. *The assumptions which make the foundations of humanism are incredible and intolerable. That the world and human life are products of chance, that man emerged from the slime simply by the blind operation of secondary causes, that he and his habitat are doomed to ultimate extinction, that there is no explanation, no justification, no purpose: all this is quite incredible, and if it had to be believed would be intolerable.*

This is a powerful objection, and no doubt one which makes many Christians believers. A powerful objection, however, because people jump to conclusions rather than because at the end of the day reflection has to admit that its weight is immovable. Rhetorical phrases like 'emergence from the slime' and 'blind chance' are less impressive after a patient study of what is meant by the biological evolution of the human species. The standard of what is credible and what incredible is not to be immediately established by untutored expectations, for it is a result of research, of establishing what has happened and what does happen. Man is a question? So is the beetle, and in the same sense. To say that it is incredible that the higher can have emerged from the lower by chance is simply a refusal, for whatever reasons, to follow the long attempt to trace what has emerged from what and how. Only in this context of research are the meaning of chance and the limited part played by chance made intelligible. The way things are as revealed by science crosses preconceptions and accustomed desires and hopes. The way things are as revealed by theology crosses the findings of investigation and the human notion of justice. Objections are matched by objections, incredibility by incredibility, intolerableness by intolerableness. Each alternative is an escape from the scandal and horrors of the other. The humanist cannot bring himself to the religious posture of unbelief and refusal which become faith and obedience.

2. *Are humanists atheists or are they really agnostic?*

As they assume that man is on his own and this life is all, humanists are virtually atheists, since practical decisions have to be made for the conduct of life. But the mind that is initiating further experience and is open to further evidence is really agnostic. There is an essential combination of practical atheism with an agnostic temper in humanism, as there may be an essential combination of agnostic surrender with theistic trust in some religious belief. The dogmatists on both sides are inert in their beliefs and their lives.

3. *Why should it be assumed that the onus is on the believer to show that his beliefs have to be taken seriously? Why should the onus not be on the unbeliever to show that the world is indeed self-explanatory and self-justifying in a way that makes religious beliefs gratuitous?*

Indeed the onus used to lie on the unbeliever when it was assumed that natural theology proved the primary truths of religion which explained and justified the world. When it was demonstrated that reason is not competent to establish the primary truths of religion, the believer had to show that nevertheless his beliefs had to be taken seriously. Now, it is sometimes suggested, he can do this best by pointing to the inadequacy of natural causes and requiring the unbeliever to justify his position.

In effect this is a demand that the unbeliever shall prove that the natural world does not need a rational and moral author because it is itself a rational and moral order. Thus the believer is asking the unbeliever to show that his unbelief is rational by restoring natural theology which reason has destroyed. The collapse of natural theology means that the obligation to justify his position has shifted from the unbeliever to the believer and cannot be bounced back. The theologian may argue that human rationality and morality imply a cosmic rational and moral order. The unbeliever is then required to show that the argument is unconvincing. But it is absurd to require him to establish an argument of this kind himself to warrant his unbelief. The onus is inescapably on the believer. That is the justification of agnosticism.

4. *Humanism is for intellectuals only. It is far too sophisticated for ordinary people.*

The small element of truth in this objection is that the philosophically minded are equipped to cope with the intellectual difficulties of belief and disbelief, and humanism starts from the position of unbelief. But on this count the same objection is far stronger against Christian theology. Indeed, the difficulty of making Christianity intelligible and credible to modern man is the contemporary crisis of theology.

The difficulties involved in belief in God and in a life after death come home to quite ordinary people when they are not sustained by a tradition of unquestioning belief. Rather than spend much time and thought on puzzling questions of this kind, they easily turn to or respond to the idea of improving the world and making the best of what offers. No, its refinements may be for the few, but humanism also appeals to common sense and provides a popular philosophy of life.

5. *Humanism may be all right when things go well, but when people are in distress or in difficulties religion alone offers help*

and consolation. Humanism is a fair-weather philosophy, not for all seasons.

Certainly humanism cannot offer the help and the consolations offered by religion, for it rejects the belief that such help and such consolations are really available. Therefore humanists address themselves to organizing and improving available help. Troubles pass or are overcome, wounds are healed with time. Friends and resources within see one through. But there are difficulties and distresses which will never be overcome, which cannot pass. In this case too, acceptance and whatever amelioration and consolation or compensation may be possible come only from resources within aided and reinforced by help from outside.

People can be helped to cope with life and to make the most of their own resources. There are friends and relations, there are the social services, and within the scope of humanism there is the humanist movement itself with its groups and counsellors, in which is shared a teaching which bargains for endurance and never lets go the possibility of enjoyment. Always the available resources are inadequate, but the point here is that the humanist attitude is not helpless and hopeless, an acknowledged or a proved bankruptcy. On the contrary, there is always something to be done and more that can be done both for remedy and for prevention.

6. *Humanism is too rational. Most people do not live rationally. Humanism errs by counting too much on reason and also by neglect of emotional and imaginative needs.*

The life of reason is indeed a humanist aspiration, but what must be understood is that the life of reason necessarily means the subordination of reason to its proper uses, not an exclusive interest in verified propositions. There is a distinction between irrational and non-rational. The irrational is contrary to reason and is to be deplored and avoided. The non-rational, on the other hand, is the chief part of personal life which it is the part of reason to help us to preserve, to develop and to enjoy to increasing purpose. Friendship, as Epicurus remarked, may begin for utilitarian considerations as an insurance against life's risks, but it may ripen into something precious for its own sake beyond utility, non-rational but not irrational. Exclusion of the non-rational by the rational is the perfect case of irrationality.

7. *The humanist may be a rationalist, says perhaps the humanist himself in a reflective mood, but he is not a humanist because he is a rationalist. If he is a humanist it is because he has come to terms with himself and therefore with the world. Some deep or difficult experience of his at some time in his life is likely to have been the occasion of this. As a human being he encounters in the world greed, hatred, fear and the violence and cunning which flow from these passions. He finds them also in himself, perhaps because he has suffered an obsessive jealousy or hatred or fear. As a human being he also encounters in the world man's humanity to man and man's creative power, and these also he finds in himself, a responsive capability he can develop. Out of this experience he discovers more than he has found, a world of possibilities. Self-knowledge, self-conquest, self-transcendence, self-creation: this is not philosophy nor argument, but experience and suffering. That is to say, humanism is not a set of opinions nor a social programme, but a type of experience issuing in a personal condition. Therefore humanism has nothing to do with an organization nor with rationalism. It cannot be organized, and the profoundest humanist may well not be a rationalist.*

Of course a set of opinions that remain inert is as useless as a set of saucepans that never leave the shelf. And of course a person who has been 'humanized' by a transforming experience is likely to be a better humanist, other things being equal, than those who have not. But can one come to terms with oneself and thus with the world unless one knows what the terms are which one has to accept? To come to terms means to give up trying to make one's own terms. This ceasing to be an island, this joining the continent of other beings is a surrender of self-sufficiency, but it makes a difference whether it is an absolute surrender to God or a yielding to facts. The terms of one's relations to oneself, to others, and to events are in question. Humanism is an assessment of these terms. Acceptance would be quite different on the terms offered by Christian faith – or Stoic philosophy. A rationalist may not become a humanist, for sure, but those who can accept themselves and the world and their fellow-men because they think they have resources beyond the natural human condition, even if they behave as humanists, are not in the same position as rationalists who are humanists, and are therefore not humanists in the same sense. Rationalists who are humanists can organize to increase their resources and enable humanists in fellowship with humanists to become better humanists.

8. *Humanists are arrogant in arrogating to themselves the name 'humanist'. Surely there are Christians who are humanists, and is not Christian humanism the best kind of humanism incorporating the whole wealth of our inheritance?*

Historically, there has been a Christian humanism in the sense that medieval Christianity was leavened by the recovery and cultivation of what Erasmus called Good Letters. Remaining a Christian, indeed wishing to devote himself to sacred literature, Erasmus nevertheless rejoiced in Lucian and Terence and made it his exercise and pleasure to translate the good Greek of the one into the good Latin of the other. He had different ideas of religion from those who thought it had to be expressed in the cowl and a dull life. In his devotion to scholarship he modelled himself on Jerome, and in his cultivation of lightness and wit he joined hands with Thomas More. In all this he represented and adorned a humane and enlightened Christianity which has a good claim to be called Christian humanism.

If Christianity baptizes not merely secular literature but now also science and social reform, it would seem to have an even stronger claim to be called Christian humanism. This claim when it is made explicit is likely to state that Christianity has all that humanism has plus something more which alone makes sense of human life and gives it value.

This claim is the real arrogance, for it runs up the humanist flag on the Christian citadel without a fight, merely ignoring the issues raised by humanism, the challenge to Christian faith.

Humanism is not Christianity minus the faith – which would be an absurdity, and is a thoughtless expression. Humanism starts with a world in which Christian faith is hardly possible but which offers possibilities of other kinds. Concentration on development of these possibilities produces a wholly different world from the one in which the Christian lives. Christian faith and hope could not be superadded to this world as a desirable extra, nice if you can get it, for it would shatter this world. There cannot be a conjunction of two inconsistent ways of thinking and living. If I were led to accept the faith and hope of a Christian, my humanism would not be crowned, it would be confounded. Worse – or better – I should myself undergo a deeply disturbing change. It is too easily and foolishly supposed that the two will mix. They will not.

True, there are a few empirical Christians who believe only in the symbolical truth of the Christian doctrines, and these might reasonably be called Christian humanists. If the Christian Church were to follow this road, the answer to the question would have to be reconsidered. But the law of self-preservation, which was the first law of Nature, is likely to prevail.

9. *Few people are primarily humanists, but there are many who would go on to say, 'but also I am a humanist', meaning that they think of themselves primarily as perhaps a communist, perhaps a Christian, perhaps even an engineer, but feel that there is more than this primary profession in their human being. Or someone who has despaired of life and repudiated all allegiances and beliefs may yet conclude, 'in spite of everything I am a humanist', meaning that in despite of himself he will let life have his vote. These 'secondary' humanists, like the 'publicans and sinners' in the Gospels, are perhaps the best humanists, for without any pretence they have in them the root of the matter.*

Perhaps in the particular personal case this may be so. But

certainly they are not better humanists *because* they are secondarily and not primarily humanists.

10. *If humanists do without religion what is their motivation? Why should they be reliable citizens? Why should they not be out simply for what they can get? Even if humanists who have been brought up in a still Christian society are restrained and dependable, is it at all probable that this will continue if humanist assumptions prevail?*

This is the kind of question which humanists find hard to take seriously. No doubt religious sanctions in the form of fear of punishment and hope of reward at the hands of an almighty and all-knowing God have influenced behaviour and may still do so, but in any view this is a crude example of the stick and the carrot which rather disgraces a society than makes the necessary foundation of civilization. In theoretical argument the basis of morals if it is not religious has usually been shifted to self-interest or utility. Men live always in a society in a state of interdependence, and therefore it is in the interest of all to conform to the rules. Then the argument comes up: it may be in the general interest that I shall conform, but when I see that I can dodge the rules and get away with it, obviously it is not in my immediate interest to conform. Society often requires me to act against what I deem my own interest. There is not a snap answer to all this, but there is a sufficient answer. A substantial part of that answer is that unless a society is indeed protecting and furthering my interests I have no real part in it and no incentive to maintain it. A society in which I am exploited is an alien and hostile world to which it is hard to recognize any moral obligation. In such a case my obligation, ideally considered, is to try to change the society. But this is likely to ask too much. In any case my interests do not exist apart from a society in which I live and on which I depend and this is not merely an abstract truth but also a felt condition which comes home to me in my personal relationships and in many of my pleasures and purposes and in the pressure of public opinion. A genuine society breeds compatriotism, participation in a larger self, a pervasive sentiment nourished by the soil in which active interests thrive. Society cannot get morality on the cheap: it is a mutual pledge for mutual benefit, or it becomes something which is neither owed nor deserved, and society drifts towards dissolution. Patriotism, a loving and cultivated response to a society that deserved well, was the glory of some ancient states. A society that is held together by the fear of hell and the hope of heaven is not a company of men and women to which it would be safe or congenial to belong.

11. *Man's unconquerable enemy is himself. He is doomed by an inner contradiction, more certainly than capitalism. 'Original sin' may be a mysterious doctrine, but sin abounds in human lives and there is no remedy in humanism.*

Sin is a theological concept and is not acknowledged by the humanist. Sin is disobedience to God. Its correlative is holiness, conversion of self-will to the will of God by the grace of God. Therefore it is only by definition that man is not able to cope with sin without grace. The inadequacy of humanism from a Christian point of view is an inadequacy measured by a criterion that belongs to a system of ideas which humanists reject.

The facts of human experience from which the notions of sin and grace derive are of course stubbornly there and not to be denied. Man's inhumanity to man, the annals of evil wrought by violence and cunning, springing from envy, covetousness, pride, lethargy, sensual passion: how to bring under control in ourselves and in the world this portion of the human inheritance is the biggest and most persistent of practical questions. If there were no evidence of moral progress at all there would be no room for hope. The student of history can point to improvement in the treatment of the mentally ill, the subnormal, the handicapped, the infirm, the destitute, all the weak and helpless members of our industrial societies. There is a more rational treatment of criminals. Imperialism has had its day. The human heart has not changed. Unlimited devilry cropped out in Nazism. But enlightenment and emancipation have indeed brought some of the benefits and improvements in human behaviour and relationships which the eighteenth-century humanists looked forward to. Absolute concepts – salvation or damnation – are out of place here. The evils that abound have to be lived with as well as attacked and diminished. With modern economic development goes a systematic endeavour by tried means to raise the standard of human conduct. The outcome is not certain but the prospects in the long view encourage reasonable hopes. There are real dangers of course, which loom larger and more plainly and universally than at any other time in history. Man has been warned.

It is understandable that the stubborn tendencies to evil of which men feel themselves victims reduce them to despair, so that they come to believe that only supernatural help can set them free to move towards the better selves of their aspirations. If it is believed that God's grace is sufficient because it is the all-in-all, the sole good for which man was created, then the possession of it is the one thing needful, and possessed and assured of all possible good man is free from his self-centred interests and desires and all the schemes and stratagems into which they lead him. He becomes a beneficent source from which good flows. This transformation of the self is beyond humanist hopes, but it is not obvious that it is achieved by professed Christians; and something more modest is really available to the humanist for his personal life. It is fully open to him to enlarge and transcend himself, and not remain self-centred in any mean and narrow sense. Unless the world excites and rewards men they are apathetic and near non-existent. Lures and lusts which make men avaricious or ambitious enlarge the self by seeking to engross the world. Other responses enlarge the self through the imagination rather than the will, shifting and dispersing self-centredness. Some of the argument between Christians and humanists might profitably take this ground. If Christian doctrine were symbolizing this imaginative transformation of the self, the substance of the difference would itself be transformed.

12. *Man in the place of God, man as the measure of all things, man worship: this is not only an abomination, it is also in-*

evitably despair and doom. Humanity needs standards beyond itself and ideals beyond its own. Cut off from these, man shrinks, withers and perishes.

There is here a common misunderstanding. Man is the measure of all things simply because he is in that position and has no choice. Even if he relies upon Revelation, he does so on his own responsibility – even if he submits to the Church. Everyone is shut up in the ego-centric predicament. He can only try to get outside himself by sharing and comparing his experience with others. Agreements based on comparisons make the endeavour to establish standards. Man as the measure of all things is a sincere striving, a shared quest, far from an arrogation of arbitrary authority affronting the universe it confronts.

Man worship is a bogey idea. Who does or could worship man? His taking upon himself the heavy responsibilities which devolve upon him when he recognizes the truth of the human condition is far from self-worship. The refusal of worship, the inability to acknowledge any absolute unconditionally worthy of worship or to find God in nature or history is in no way equivalent to transferring worship of God to worship of man. The humanist's refusal of worship because the object of worship is not to be found is quite explicit. That is one reason why there is objection to calling humanism a religion: it does not retain the religious categories – the numinous, the sacred, the holy, the worshipful, the eternal, the absolute – and give them a new content. Humanism is a rejection of these categories.

Emphatically, however, this does not mean an enthronement of human pride. 'Hubris' is an anglicized Greek word for human uppishness. To use this word as a warning out of the context of Greek thinking, as is sometimes done, is as objectionable as the preservation of religious categories in which to install secular contents. The Greeks thought of the disparity between the divine and the human; for a man to take too much upon himself, not to *know himself* as human, was to invite the displeasure and the revenge of the gods. Aristotle said this was sheer superstition, for human reason made man akin to the divine, and the cultivation of reason assimilated humanity to divinity.

If man is on his own, there are no gods to ape. If reason is a human and social property, nobody can be affronted by its use, and its limits are the limits of its use, not a frontier which it is forbidden to penetrate. Man on his own must act according to his lights. Ideals are guides and goals, but they are not worshipful. In the end all is mysterious, equally 'given': everything equally. One does not therefore necessarily bow down in awe, nor render thanks in gratitude. These may be moods and modes of response. Other responses are not less appropriate, intellectual, emotional and practical. The humanist attitude to human being in any person is a settled respect grounded in the possibilities open to human being and the responsibility borne by human being. This respect for a certain condition or means is decisively different from admiration addressed to excellence or worship addressed to perfection, which are ends. This respect for the means to admirable achievement is blended with sympathy with an equal subject of suffering and enjoyment, one who is an end for himself and for others. The humanist response to the natural world in all its manifestations is acceptance in spite of rejection and rejection in spite of acceptance, an interpenetration of enjoyment and endurance in a more or less stable equilibrium. Again, this is decisively different from worship. Humanism really is an alternative to religion, in a sense in which it is not an alternative to, say, philosophy or politics.

13. *The argument about God and religious belief is otiose today. The real issues are quite different. The question which divides the sheep from the goats is not, do you or do you not believe in God and that Christ rose from the dead, but rather, are you or are you not against nuclear stockpiles, or are you against rule by an élite or not? and what are you doing about these things?*

This, in a new form, is an age-old point of view, which insists on shifting the accent of importance from ultimate questions about the nature of existence to present questions about conduct and policies, from theology to society, from creed to deed, from unanswerable questions which occasion division amongst people of goodwill to practical questions which should unite people of goodwill. Who is the enemy and where are our friends? To shift the issue to practical ground may restore a sense of proportion, and on the whole this is a humanist approach. But this common sense is often naïve. There are two points of criticism.

The questions posed as the really serious issues are liable to be posed in a way that reduces the issue to a misleading simplicity. International order may be the most serious problem of our time, but to hold up everyone on the question for or against nuclear stockpiles is not necessarily the way to separate the friends from the enemies of mankind. Perhaps there is not any question which can be used quite simply as a test of this kind in practice. There is no doubt that such questions can be used effectively as a rhetorical tactic in debate.

Secondly, ultimate convictions about God and man do affect conduct and practical decisions. If life and conduct are to be just the same with or without belief in God, obviously the belief has ceased to matter – and that is the assumption of the present objection, that belief makes no real difference to the behaviour of modern people. The humanist does not think this. He would say that active belief or active humanism makes all the difference in the world, not the difference between responsible and irresponsible conduct, nor the difference between one view and another of nuclear weapons or of government by an *élite*, but the difference between a life of obedience and a life of self-creation.

14. *Humanists are individualists. They do not agree. Therefore humanism is a name about nothing.*

All right, they are individualists and they do not agree on many things. But they do not have to agree except on their basic assumptions about human life, their methods of getting informed about it, and their responsibilities for it. And on these matters they are agreed. By definition they do not have to agree about personal choices and private lives. They may well differ on political policies. There are disagreements within the sciences, and there are procedures for resolving them. There are disagreements under monolithic regimes like the Roman Church and Communist parties, and there are procedures for resolving them. Humanism is not different from these in holding together people who have disagreements, but it is less exacting in the agreement it requires in order to bring people together with a sense of sharing fundamentals and with the purpose of learning from one another and of doing together what they want to see done in the world. The preliminary assumptions, the humanist tradition, the actual organization, the programme, the aims and objects: these manifestly exist, so that there really is something which can be called humanism. I suppose most people who call themselves humanists would agree in the main with the contents of this book. But if they thought they had to think it infallible, if they could not disagree with it, they would fall into violent disagreement about it.

15. *To keep an open mind is too difficult for most people. They can't live with uncertainty. They want to know what to think and how to live, not be put off with evasive answers and thrown back on themselves.*

There are systems of thought and there are established authorities that do just this, tell people what to think and how to live. Those who must have this can get it. The humanist will not hand over his own responsibility in this way because he does not think that the certainty claimed by established authorities or for total systems of thought is to be had. He thinks that people who accept these certainties and live by them are deceiving themselves and being deceived.

However, the need for certainty and the quest for certainty are habits of mind. They are learned in a culture which is based at bottom on some absolute. We can certainly learn to live with uncertainty as a matter of course. But we could never live with blank uncertainty, not knowing what to expect, with no dependable experience. This state of affairs, if it were possible, could produce only paralysis and collapse. Obviously, mankind would never have come into existence without some dependable order of experience. Science is built on this. Living with uncertainty means in practice living with the most dependable knowledge we can have, which is never beyond question and always subject to modification and development with further experience and in new contexts. Knowledge which claims to be absolutely certain is cut off from the source and meaning and use of knowledge.

16. *The open society cannot be foisted on others by humanists. Unless and until the great majority are humanists, it is merely a humanist idea. And how can it be open if it does not and cannot tolerate those who want a society based on an absolute?*

The precondition of an open society is the admitted existence of differences about the ultimates of conviction. Then the absolute is denied absolute rights even by the absolutists, on condition that their right to try to convince their fellow citizens is not denied. The seventeenth-century principle that the magistrate has no jurisdiction over conscience and the nineteenth-century contention that democratic majorities have no jurisdiction over private lives (Locke's *A Letter Concerning Toleration* and Mill's *On Liberty*) are the rough-hewn lineaments of the open society, and they were hewn out of hard experience, not figured fancifully on paper.

17. *The humanist himself, living a life of his own, following his own choices, is a nice idea, but it can be only a dream for most people. Their chances of escaping from the prison of circumstances and the daily grind of breadwinning are pretty slim, even in affluent societies.*

Humanism as a practical movement is wholly addressed to this problem of creating the conditions for all of a life worthy to be called human, of instituting a human providence. This can be attempted only by political and social action and by education. The individual has to help himself, but he has first to be enabled to help himself. To say that in principle human beings never can enjoy the humanist ideal of personal fulfilment or that only a few lucky and gifted people in any generation will ever be able to do it is to ignore the means proposed or to judge them totally inadequate. Humanists do not think that there is enough experience yet of what can be done to justify any such conclusive judgement.

18. *Humanism is materialistic. It reduces man to a physical organism. The soul and the human spirit, all that is distinctively human, is left out. Humanism belies its name.*

Humanism *is* materialistic, but not in this sense. It is materialistic in the sense of *referring* everything to some material organization on which it is ultimately dependent, but not in the sense of *reducing* everything to its material substratum. The violin performance of a work is not dismissed as the rubbing of hair on gut, nor an experience of another kind as a friction of skins. Materialism is the condition of dependable knowledge, fulfillable purpose, and of every lively and lovely experience. The soul does not leave the body and does not survive the body, and is the body in the sense that this is a name for possibilities of use and enjoyment which this body, the human body, is known to have.

Man can be studied as an object, and is reduced to an object for this purpose; but this is man, not you nor me. My inner temporal life, with its hold on the present, its support from the past, and its reach into the future is the most real and interesting aspect of me to myself and to others. Idealism roots and flourishes best in the good cultivable dirt of materialism continually replenished with organic waste and decay. Humanism is this fertile combination of materialism and idealism. The only opposition between the two is when they become philosophic doctrines: all is matter; all is idea. (The fierce age-old controversy summed up in the witty gibe: What is mind? No matter. What is matter? Never mind.)

The human spirit exists and is seen to exist in its achievements, which are many-sided. Man is all that he is found to be. Perhaps humanists have been in the past too often one-sided. They have been rationalists (scientific humanism). They have been moralists (ethical humanism). They have been secularists (secular humanism). They stood for science against obscurantists, for democracy against oligarchies and despots, for autonomous morality when theology seemed to be on the way out, for the arts when the arts had been too long neglected or restricted, to some extent they stood for the inner life at the time of the romantic revival and in connexion with psychoanalysis. These phases of intense concentration on an exclusive ideal in response to prevailing conditions which excluded it have been necessary but costly, for they have produced types of humanism which are rigid and one-sided, and fall short of the full humanist ideal. In this sense humanism may have belied its name and has reduced man. But it has been idealism and for the sake of man, not materialism and in despite of man.

19. *Humanism as a certain position, especially in relation to traditional religion, is understandable and perhaps inevitable. But why an organized movement? This, surely, must have the effect of establishing humanism as another sect? Humanism may be a desirable escape from religion: must it harden into the obverse of religion?*

This argument would make of humanism merely a set of private opinions in one's head. Such opinions are hardly worth having if those who have them leave others with different views to exert influence and organize the world. Some opinions, including some that are distinctively humanist, do not call for a party. But a total concern for the conditions of human life, which humanism is, means joint action or cant. The argument against organization reflects a very partial understanding of what humanism is about, which amounts to misunderstanding.

All the same, there is an ever-present danger that organized humanism will harden into a sect. Especially when the organization is based on a one-sided ideal (rationalism or secularism or autonomous ethics) is there a heavy liability to rigidity. These are partial and imperfect forms of organization for the total concern which humanism properly is. The bringing together of national organizations with different starting points and outlooks into a world organization, International Humanist and Ethical Union, has begun and will continue to enlarge the horizons and liberate the spirit of organized humanism. But there remains always in organization the liability to rigidity and to idolatries. The Christian Church is a classical warning.

20. *How militant is organized humanism? Is it out to extirpate religious faith, and is it organized in opposition to the churches?*

The existence of organized religion in missionary churches necessarily involves organized humanism in opposition. The churches seek to extend their influence; they contend for the young; they can hardly be ignored. There are unavoidably fronts of public argument in which Christians and humanists are opponents. The liberals on both sides, friends of the open mind and the open society, are bound to find that they have a great deal in common. In principle, humanists should all be liberals in this sense whereas Christians may not be. But human beings in the flesh are liable to self-contradiction, and sometimes project their own problems and failures on others.

Humanists may think that believers are deceived, and wish and work for a world without religion – indeed, they must; but in practice they would not want to rob believers of their faith, especially when they are no longer young. This may be contradictory, but there are other considerations in the case besides logic. Should a doctor tell? Perhaps, but this is his patient who has come to consult him and whom he knows. To go up to somebody in the Underground and tell him that he has manifest symptoms of a fatal disease because you are a doctor and you know is quite another matter. The open mind means acceptance of fallibility. The open heart means acceptance of humanity. I have known a militant secularist suffer sharp and lasting regret for the obtrusion of his views on an old lady casually met whose faith was the prop as well as the propriety of her life.

21. *What can humanist parents tell their children? Are they not at a great disadvantage compared with Christian parents in a*

Christian society? In any case, is there anything they can give their children to stand them in good stead throughout life? What positive foundation can they provide?

This is a searching question, and conscientious humanist parents are liable to get worried. On the other hand, humanism appeals to some parents as the very thing to give their children anchorage in an age of unsettlement and drift.

The first part of an answer is that the experience parents give a child does more harm than good than anything that is said nor not said. That experience comes from the way the child is treated and the way the parents behave and live. A child who enjoys affection, understanding, interest and never-failing encouragement, without being left to be ruled by his own drives or allowed to rule the house, will have favourable soil in which to root and thrive. Bertrand Russell's dictum, 'Never punish, never give way', is the counsel of perfection. Parents' own behaviour should include complete honesty about their views and the manifest attempt to live in the light of them.

Children are at times more influenced by their peers than by their parents, and it is usually wise to let them join the groups their friends belong to, which are quite likely to be sponsored by churches. This need not worry humanist parents unduly so long as the child is fully aware of the views that prevail at home and is encouraged to air his own ideas, and so long as he knows that his parents belong to a respectable company in the views they hold and are not cranky. Quite young children in the first decade of life are natural anthropologists interested in the diversity of views and behaviour around them. This is the age at which they should become acquainted with such differences. If the adults hold in respect others with different views and ways, there is no strain nor stress, for at this time no decisions have to be made. As the years go on parents can help to extend and deepen this acquaintance with the diverse patterns of human belief. (Help can be found in the Pelican book, *A Short History of Religions* by E. E. Kellett.) It is fair for humanist parents to insist both on the good and on the evil for which religion has been responsible in history. It is fair also to protest against the official pretence that this is a Christian country.

Morally, the fundamental thing is respect for human being in every person including oneself as autonomous and responsible. With this goes respect for rational standards in forming opinions and making decisions. With this self-dependence goes recognition of interdependence and acceptance of the conditions of coexistence and cooperation. Awareness of and response to the needs of others is as normal and approved as respect for their human dignity. Giving sense and value to all is the enjoyment of a personal life of one's own. If a child is enabled in due course to grasp for himself the moral perspective indicated in these sentences he is prepared for the difficulties, the calamities, the temptations he is likely to encounter on his way through life. But this is not something he can just be told. He can learn it in the family by experience, by example, by discussion. Parents may need or profit by some help, but there is no substitute for themselves and no avoidance of the influence of what they are and how they live. If they do endow their children with the moral equipment to see them through life, their memory will be blessed for the most valuable possible legacy. Humanist families are the richest in these resources.

22. *The eighteenth-century humanists proclaimed not only the Rights of Man but also the Reign of Man, the progress of mankind and the perfectibility of the species. Since then, however, thinkers have been disillusioned. Modern utopias are nightmares. How can humanists restore confidence and the courage to live if indeed 'Man is the future of man'?*

The supposed unqualified optimism of eighteenth-century humanists is a lie perpetrated by the enemies of humanism. Like Bacon before them they were concerned to give men new confidence by giving them new methods and a new vision. Bacon based his appeal for confidence on the new methods of science which promised progressive knowledge to be applied to the relief of man's estate. Condorcet based his appeal on the method of changing human behaviour by changing social institutions, and on the cumulative effect of inter-related advances. Both Bacon and Condorcet have been proved essentially right. The resources with which to tackle human problems have been tremendously expanded: the problems, new and old, are correspondingly big. If some basis of world order and security can be established, if population growth can be checked, if the developing peoples can be aided to the point of self-development, if the mixed economies can be managed and the communist states can get nearer to their ideal of withering away, the general prospect for mankind will have been transformed. These appear to be very big 'ifs', but indeed the 'cans' are already fully possible and the ifs really depend upon 'wills'. Even so, the future is by no means easy nor certain – and nobody thinks that it is.

Knowing the way or knowing how to learn to know the way is the main key to confidence and courage. A vision of the better possibility which is the transformation of the human situation open to mankind, and a lively sense of what the worse possibilities are, help to nerve people to the resolution and persistence required for success. A humanist movement that helps people to be socially effective and personally in possession of themselves, creators of their own experience, goes to the root of the matter. To see what to do and to go about doing it is the highest satisfaction, and the only reasonable way of avoiding worry about what will happen.

23. *Nevertheless, in the long run, on humanist assumptions, it is only a prolonged agony of futility, 'a tale told by an idiot'. The humanist, who will not bend a knee in acknowledgement of any absolute, must succumb to the final absolute, the dark oblivion that awaits him and will in due course obliterate every track and trace of human being. That absolute oblivion in which whatever has been will be as though it never had been is the unthinkable absolute which the humanist chooses in denying the living Absolute, which is also unthinkable but which remains the better possibility chosen by the believer. Humanism, for all its genial assurances and the appearance of monumental solidity, is a butterfly existence. Why this chosen*

irredeemable pessimism, this nihilism? There is a wiser alternative.

Smooth words in defence of a fixed position will not blot up this rhetoric, for, however it is put, this last objection is the final protest against humanism, the refusal which many people find not only in their hearts or stomachs but also in their heads. Rationalism which leads to the abyss is the supreme folly.

The loved detail of a landscape is annihilated by distance, but one can return and find it. There is no return in time, but what once was somewhere had no less reality than what is elsewhere. The loves and achievements, the tragedies and comedies swallowed up with the empire of Xerxes were as real as our own, and as those of yesterday which have passed into equal oblivion. By the criterion of eventual oblivion there are no distinctions nor standards, no virtues nor values nor joys nor sorrows: nothing is. This is the true nihilism, to take oblivion as the measure of all things because oblivion may be the destiny of all things. To accept and respect the temporal condition of all things is the beginning of wisdom, for this is the condition and source of all the things that we love and long for, and we can really think of no other terms on which we could enjoy them nor exist ourselves to enjoy them. To appeal against the temporal terms of the human condition, the ephemeral character of our life, to aspire to an eternal unconditioned existence is not really to look for salvation, for it is to reject and forfeit life. This earnest refusal of life is the profoundest thoughtlessness, the tragic misunderstanding not merely of the terms of human existence but mainly of its very character, what there is there to love and care for, and how it is as it is. Thought abstracts from the web of actual conditions and imagines the impossible, unless corrected by further thought.

Is this, then, the best of all possible worlds, even if a sorry scheme of things? Impossible to answer, for we have no means of judging what is possible except by what is. But however sorry the scheme is we sometimes bless it with all our heart and all our mind and all our strength. That we can do so and that we cannot always do so is the state of affairs, the reality with which we live, the enjoyment–endurance continuum which is the medium of our art. Those who are living to some purpose are concerned with a time-scale they can manage which bears their own hopes and fears, and they leave the irrelevant long future of oblivion to take care of itself. The verdict, All is vanity, is the unforgivable blasphemy, the threshold of higher religion. The Epicurean radical discouragement of the absurd lust for immortality in this world or thereafter is the beginning of self-containment which is the threshold to an accurate appreciation and unclouded enjoyment of the things of this world, with or without possession. It will be said at once that 'unclouded enjoyment' is just what we do not have. True, if one is thinking of an impossible paradise; wickedly untrue if one is denying the pure unalloyed small enjoyments which colour the day. When one becomes incapable of these it is time to die.

Francis Bacon has been described as a religious painter working in an atheistic age. Because he is an unbeliever he is preoccupied with the animality of man and the futility of everything: art is distraction because there is nothing to celebrate. He has also been described as a humanist because his whole interest is in the human figure, the personal image, and he sees in abstracts a limited interest which is merely aesthetic. Similarly, Jean-Paul Sartre may be described as a rationalist philosopher dismayed by a non-rational natural world. And he calls his existentialism a humanism. Both these contemporaries have their rights, and they may be representative and speak for many. But it would be quite wrong to think that they are the honest humanists, and that all other humanists in so far as they are honest with themselves will be driven logically or psychologically to similar positions and attitudes of typical dismay. On the contrary, it can be firmly and fairly said in the light of the humanist tradition that these are distorted or immature forms of humanist expression, perhaps a result of anguished misunderstanding induced by centuries of Christian faith. (One can say this and still give full marks to Sartre for his demonstration of political and human concern.)

But can humanists really and justifiably maintain equanimity in the face not only of probable ultimate annihilation but also of actual human suffering and stupidity and brutality on the present scale? Is there any satisfaction at all to be found in the general behaviour of mankind or in the trends and tendencies that can be discerned? There is no answer to such a question, or no general answer, for there is no general behaviour of mankind. Everybody must balance his own account here. In any such reckoning, the ready money of daily cheerfulness and unalloyed pleasures is not too small to count. One dimension of finality is here and now. On the public fronts, defeatism may sometimes be the part of reason acting as prudence, but who will responsibly say that the time is now? So long as there are better and worse possibilities there is time for action. Today the better and the worse are better and worse than they have ever been. That is the summons to humanists and the summons of humanism.

FURTHER READING

GEORGE SANTAYANA published in 1905–6 *The Life of Reason, or The Phases of Human Progress*, a subtle, perceptive, imaginative survey of human life, beautifully composed. In the last year of his life, with the help of Daniel Cory, he abridged and revised this work for a one-volume edition (Constable, 1954). This is the most comprehensive contemplative humanism. Santayana was 'deficient in the most material part of virtue', 'a regard to the community', a conspicuous part of the humanism of other Americans, like one of his students, Walter Lippmann, whose own early book *A Preface to Morals* (Allen & Unwin, 1929) was an essay in orientation for the young intelligentsia in the confusion after collapse in authority and tradition. John Dewey, apostle of science and democracy, proclaimed his humanist faith in many notable books. His Terry Lectures *A Common Faith* (Yale University Press, 1934) give his views on religion in a statement of humanist conviction. Earlier, Julian Huxley had combined a positive critique of religion with a claim for humanism as heir to the historical faiths in *Religion Without Revelation* (1927). A third revised edition ('New Thinker's Library', Watts, 1967) forty years later contains a full exposition of Huxley's 'Evolutionary Humanism'. He has described his brother Aldous as 'the greatest humanist of our time'. There can be no doubt that many of the early essays are a repudiation of 'high moralities' as 'a most discreditable admission that you lack the guts, the wit, the moderating judgement to be successfully and consummately human'; particularly, the collection *Do What You Will* (Chatto & Windus, 1929). The ecstasy of natural living is memorably expressed by Llewelyn Powys in books probably now forgotten and hard to come by (*Glory of Life* and *Now That the Gods are Dead*, Bodley Head, 1949; *Impassioned Clay*, Longmans, 1931). A more sober academic defence of humanist values on all fronts is Richard Robinson's *An Atheist's Values* (Oxford, 1964). Bertrand Russell, who has touched life at many points as a good humanist should, might be represented by *The Conquest of Happiness* (Allen & Unwin, 1930); *Let the People Think* (Barrie & Rockcliff, 1950).

Corliss Lamont, a philosopher active in the American Humanist Association, and a warm admirer of Santayana, published in 1949 a systematic presentation of humanism as a philosophy. With a changed title, this has been revised and reprinted several times, and is now available in a fifth edition (*The Philosophy of Humanism*, Barrie & Rockliff, 1957). Lamont also wrote *The Illusion of Immortality*, with an Introduction by John Dewey, republished in a fourth edition thirty years later (Frederick Ungar, New York, 1965). Hector Hawton, editor of the monthly magazine *Humanist*, has written a notably readable account of humanism as a philosophy of life (*The Humanist Revolution*, Barrie & Rockliff, 1963). *What Humanism is About* by Kit Mouat (Barrie & Rockliff, 1963), although the title is rather a misnomer, is a readable popular introduction to the humanist approach to present questions – and is a woman's approach that is always mindful of a woman's point of view.

Sir Julian Huxley brought in twenty-five other contributors in *The Humanist Frame* (Allen & Unwin, 1961), and himself contributed a major statement of his own Evolutionary Humanism. Professor Ayer is editing another collection, contributed by members of the Advisory Council of the British Humanist Association, *The Humanist Outlook*, to be published by Barrie & Rockliff early in 1968. Proceedings of the Congresses of the International Humanist and Ethical Union have been published for the four Congresses from the headquarters of IHEU in Utrecht. Also issued by IHEU (1957) is a valuable survey of humanist schools of thought, *Humanism* by Professor J. P. van Praag, the Chairman. In the four essays in *Objections to Humanism* which I edited (Constable, 1963; Pelican, 1965) humanists look critically at their humanism and take seriously objections to their position. There is a preliminary statement of the position in an introductory essay. Margaret Knight has compiled *Humanist Anthology, From Confucius to Bertrand Russell* (Barrie & Rockliff, 1961).

The general principle of the 'open society' is best studied in Sir Karl Popper's *The Open Society and its Enemies*, published in two volumes in 1945 (Routledge Paperback). Relevant from the Christian side are J. N. Figgis: *Churches in the Modern State* (Longmans, 1913), and D. L. Munby: *The Idea of a Secular Society, And its Significance for Christians* (Riddell Lectures, 1962), an opposition to T. S. Eliot's *The Idea of a Christian Society* (Faber, 1939). The arguments are fully discussed in my

Religion in a Modern Society (Constable, 1966). The political meaning of an open society is brilliantly brought out by Professor Bernard Crick: *In Defence of Politics* (Pelican, 1963, revised 1964).

A humanist critique of society in the Ruskin spirit has a noble literature. Lewis Mumford's *The Culture of Cities* (Secker & Warburg, 1938) is the chief modern exemplar, one of many works in which he expresses his rich civic humanism.

Characteristic humanist approaches to social study, social philosophy and social service are represented by: *Testament for Social Science, An Essay in the Application of Scientific Method to Human Problems* by Barbara Wootton (Allen & Unwin, 1959); *On Justice in Society* by Morris Ginsberg (Pelican, 1966); *Waste. An Eye-Witness Report on Some Aspects of Waste in Western Sicily* by Danilo Dolci (MacGibbon & Kee, 1963); *The Fraternal Society* by Richard and Hephzibah Hauser (Bodley Head, 1962); *Yes to Life* by James Hemming (Nelson, 1967); *Religious Education in State Schools* by Brigid Brophy (Fabian Tract 374, 1967); *Religion in State-aided Schools in England and Wales* (British Humanist Association, 1967).

Ethics is an independent theoretical study of moral phenomena, but moral theory may have a humanist foundation – or not. R. Osborn in *Humanism and Moral Theory* (Allen & Unwin, 1959) sets out to provide the theory that can rationally justify characteristic humanist condemnations of such evils as race segregation, or economic and social exploitation. P. H. Nowell-Smith sees personal responsibility for the choice of moral principles as the main meaning of morality: *Ethics* (Pelican, 1954). Margaret Knight's *Morals Without Religion* reproduces her famous broadcasts. Professor C. H. Waddington's *The Ethical Animal* (Allen & Unwin, 1960) is the mature statement of an evolutionary view of the nature and importance of ethics. Morris Ginsberg's essay 'On the Diversity of Morals' in the volume of papers with that title (Heinemann, 1956) analyses the progress of morals from relativity to universality. Erich Fromm's *Man for Himself, An Enquiry into the Psychology of Ethics* (Routledge & Kegan Paul, 1949) is also a refutation of ethical relativism, and a reaffirmation of humanistic ethics after disillusionment with the hopes of the Enlightenment. Erik H. Erikson goes deeper in *Insight and Responsibility, Lectures on the Ethical Implications of Psychoanalytic Insight* (Faber, 1966). *Psychoanalysis Observed* edited by Charles Rycroft (Constable,

1966) is an important revaluation of psychoanalysis as a contribution to the humanization of man in society.

Karl Jasper's essay 'Philosophy and Science', should be read on the open mind. It is reprinted in my *Reality, Man and Existence* (Bantam Books, 1965). The basis and validity of empirical knowledge, the question of certainty, and the nature of philosophy are discussed by A. J. Ayer in *The Problem of Knowledge* (Pelican, 1956). The grounds of humanist rejection of religious dogma are given in Professor Ronald Hepburn's *Christianity and Paradox, Critical Studies in Twentieth Century Theology* (Watts, 1958) and Professor Antony Flew's *God and Philosophy* (Hutchinson, 1966). Professor Hepburn is in discussion with theologians in *Religion and Humanism* (B.B.C., 1964).

Humanism and the arts has a small but interesting literature, which throws light on the nature of humanism. To begin with architecture, which has its source model in the human body (Michelangelo said it derives from the limbs of men), Geoffrey Scott's *The Architecture of Humanism* (Constable, 1914; Methuen University Paperback, 1960) takes the history of ideas as the spine of the history of taste and appraises the architecture of man when he *was* 'at home in the world'. To create an environment in which man *can* be at home is the theme of a work on contemporary architecture: *Community and Privacy, Towards a New Architecture of Humanism* by Serge Chermayeff and Christopher Alexander (New York, 1963; Pelican, 1966). In painting and sculpture, *The Age of Humanism, 1480–1530*, by André Chastel (Thames & Hudson, 1963). An ingenious and learned study of the parallel between ideas and painting is Leo Balet's *Rembrandt and Spinoza* (New York, Philosophical Library, 1962). One of Santayana's best books is *Three Philosophical Poets: Lucretius, Dante and Goethe*. The impact of Renaissance humanism and the new science of the seventeenth century on poetry has been studied by M. M. Mahood in *Poetry and Humanism* (Cape, 1950).

The Humanist tradition is a library in itself; but one or two books can be picked for each of the main periods. For the Greeks: *In the Beginning: Some Greek Views on the Origins of Life and the Early State of Man* by W. K. C. Guthrie (Methuen, 1957); *Four Stages of Greek Thought* by John H. Finley, Jr. (Oxford, 1966); *Humanism, The Greek Ideal and its Survival* by Moses Hadas (Allen & Unwin, 1960); *Epicurus and his*

Philosophy by Norman Wentworth de Witt (Minneapolis & London, 1954). For the Renaissance: *Eight Philosophers of the Italian Renaissance* by Paul Oskar Kristeller (Chatto & Windus, 1965); *The Crisis of the Early Italian Renaissance, Civic Humanism and Republican Liberty in an Age of Classicism and Tyranny* by Hans Baron (2 vols. 1955; revised one-volume edition, Princeton Paperbacks, 1966). For the Enlightenment: *The Philosophy of the Enlightenment* by Ernst Cassirer (German ed. 1932; English translation, Princeton, Mayflower Paperback, 1951); *French Liberal Thought in the 18th Century, A Study of Political Ideas from Bayle to Condorcet* by Kingsley Martin (1929; Revised ed. by J. P. Mayer, Turnstile Press, 1954). *The Growth of Philosophical Radicalism* by Elie Halévy (1901–14) of which there is a one-volume translation by Mary Morris (Faber, 1928) is a valuable study of the origins, principles, methods, objects and achievements of the English reformers. *Matthew Arnold and John Stuart Mill* by Edward Alexander (Routledge & Kegan Paul, 1965) is 'an attempt to show the confluence of humanism and liberalism as a preparation for democracy'. Two general histories: *The History of Materialism* by F. A. Lange (1865; one volume, edited and with Introduction by Bertrand Russell, Routledge & Kegan Paul, 1950); *A History of Freedom of Thought* by J. B. Bury (Home University Library, 1913; second edition with an Epilogue by H. J. Blackham, 1952). A spirited review and reaffirmation of the modern humanist tradition is *The Case for Modern Man* by Charles Frankel (Macmillan, 1957). Another humanist revaluation: *The Idea of Progress, A Revaluation* by Morris Ginsberg (Methuen, 1953).

As distinct from the specific humanist tradition, a global view of man, his past, his knowledge, his task, is characteristic of the humanist outlook. H. G. Wells's *The Outline of History* (Cassell, 1923) is the modern prototype, followed by Ritchie Calder in *The Inheritors, The Story of Man and the World He Made* (Heinemann, 1961). An impressive attempt to inform the present role of man by the lessons of history is *The Uses of the Past, Profiles of Former Societies* by Herbert J. Muller (1952; a Galaxy Book, 1957). An attempt to get perspective in terms of knowledge and development is *The Changing Mind* by John Roddam (Cape, 1966).

Finally, the making of a humanist and humanist thinking and living can be agreeably and profitably studied in autobiography and biography. There are many brilliant examples. Let two suffice here: *The Autobiography of Bertrand Russell, 1872–1914* (Allen & Unwin, 1967); *The Life and Work of Sigmund Freud* by Ernest Jones (edited and abridged by Lionel Trilling and Steven Marcus, Pelican, 1964).

There are two comprehensive bibliographies of Humanism: *A Guide to Humanist Books in English* by H. J. Blackham (The Plain View Supplements I, London, 1955); *Bibliography of Humanism* by Kwee Swan Liat (Humanist League, Utrecht, 1957). The first, now out of print but available in some libraries, is annotated, with short introductions to the sections.

This note on further reading is far from exhaustive, but the books that have been listed represent a copious, rich and diverse literature of humanism that already exists, and is growing.

INDEX